OSPREY COMBAT AIRCRAFT • 97

USAF AND VNAF A-1 SKYRAIDER UNITS OF THE VIETNAM WAR

SERIES EDITOR: TONY HOLMES

OSPREY COMBAT AIRCRAFT • 97

USAF AND VNAF A-1 SKYRAIDER UNITS OF THE VIETNAM WAR

BYRON E HUKEE

OSPREY
PUBLISHING

Front Cover
On 12 June 1972, 1Lt Byron Hukee and his wingman Capt Gene Bardal of the 1st Special Operations Squadron (SOS) were scrambled from search and rescue (SAR) ground alert at Da Nang Air Base (AB), in South Vietnam, as 'Sandy 07' and 'Sandy 08'. 'Jolly Green 65' and '21', a flight of two HH-53 rescue helicopters, launched with the 'Sandys'. The SAR forces were told that there was a US Army OH-6, call-sign 'Blue Ghost 10', down about 18 nautical miles west-southwest of Hue. A 'Covey' Forward Air Controller (FAC) in the SAR area had no contact with any potential survivors. He reported that two other helicopters had been lost the preceding day in the same area.

'Sandy 08' directed the Jolly Greens to hold 'feet wet' east of Hue, while leading his flight into the SAR area. 'Covey' reported seeing mirror flashes close to a smoking crash site near the Song Ba River. 'Sandy 07' assumed on scene command, directing 'Sandy 08' to stay high and be alert for SA-7 missile launches while he entered the area to search for possible survivors.

Hukee, in A-1J 142028, assessed the threats in the area and returned enemy ground fire with a portion of his ordnance. During this time he too saw mirror flashes originating from near the crash site. Repeated attempts at radio contact proved futile. Was it a trap, or were there Americans down there who needed rescuing?

Bardal, in A-1H 139791, was sent to bring the Jolly Greens closer to the SAR area, after which 'Sandy 07' briefed the team on his SAR plan. His instincts told him that there were survivors to be rescued, but if it were a trap, the 'Sandys' would position themselves to immediately suppress enemy fire, while directing the Jolly Greens to abort the pickup. Both 'Sandys' would lay down a smoke screen to shield the Jolly Greens from possible threats. The Jolly Greens were directed to proceed inbound as fast as possible in order to minimise the effectiveness of threats en route to the survivor.

The SAR team executed the plan flawlessly. A Jolly Green pararescue jumper (PJ) was lowered to assist a badly injured crewmember into the helicopter – the other crewmember had been killed when the OH-6 crashed. 'Jolly Green 65' egressed the area, escorted by Hukee and Bardal, and flew the survivor to Da Nang AB (*Cover art by Mark Postlethwaite*)

First published in Great Britain in 2013 by Osprey Publishing
Midland House, West Way, Botley, Oxford, OX2 0PH
43-01 21st Street, Suite 220B, Long Island City, NY 11101, USA

E-mail; info@ospreypublishing.com

Osprey Publishing is part of the Osprey Group

A CIP catalogue record for this book is available from the British Library

ISBN: 978 1 78096 068 5
PDF ebook ISBN: 978 1 78096 069 2
ePub ISBN: 978 1 78096 070 8

Edited by Tony Holmes
Cover Artwork by Mark Postlethwaite
Aircraft Profiles by Jim Laurier
Originated by PDQ Digital Media Solutions, Suffolk, UK
Index by Alan Thatcher
Printed in China through Bookbuilders

13 14 15 17 17 10 9 8 7 6 5 4 3 2 1

Osprey Publishing is supporting the Woodland Trust, the UK's leading woodland conservation charity, by funding the dedication of trees.

www.ospreypublishing.com

CONTENTS

INTRODUCTION

To cover the units that flew Skyraiders in both the USAF and the Vietnamese Air Force (VNAF) during the Vietnam War proved to be a somewhat daunting task. The 12 squadrons of these two air forces that were equipped with the Douglas aircraft saw extensive combat from 1960 to 1975. And this 15-year period is but five years short of spanning the entire existence of the VNAF. History will show that with the introduction of the AD-6 Skyraider in 1960, the VNAF truly had a capable, albeit demanding, aircraft – demanding in that it required a pilot's full attention all of the time, whether in the air or on the ground. That it lasted 15 years as the VNAF's frontline attack aircraft speaks volumes for its capabilities, and those of the men who flew it.

These capabilities, however, did not come without a price. Of the approximately 350 Skyraiders operated by the VNAF, only 70 remained by the end of 1973. And by the time the North Vietnamese Army (NVA) invaded South Vietnam in April 1975, just 40 Skyraiders were left at various VNAF bases for the enemy to use as they saw fit. It was the end of not only the VNAF, but also of the country the Skyraider units had fought so hard to defend.

Nestled inside this 15-year timeframe was the eight-year period that the USAF operated various models of the A-1 Skyraider in Southeast Asia. Commencing operations in-theatre in mid-1964, Skyraiders were the premier close air support (CAS) aircraft for the USAF until the end of 1972.

This map shows the location of USAF and VNAF bases from which A-1 Skyraider units operated during the conflict in Southeast Asia

The A-1 also became synonymous with the search and rescue (SAR) mission, and many a downed airman gave thanks when he heard the voice of a 'Sandy' on his survival radio, followed shortly after by the din of the Wright R-3350 radial engine as the Skyraider roared overhead. But make no mistake, the A-1 served well in all of its roles, from Special Forces fort defence to Military Assistance Command, Vietnam – Studies and Observations Group (MACV-SOG) support.

All Skyraider pilots gave some, but far too many gave their all. Of the approximately 330 A-1s operated by the USAF in Southeast Asia, nearly 200 were lost. More than 100 USAF Skyraider pilots were either killed in action or listed as missing in action.

To help the reader remain oriented, a map of Southeast Asian air bases is shown opposite. A Skyraider unit timeline is provided in the Appendix.

Within each chapter, total losses of Skyraiders and pilots are given. This data comes from military and government sources for both the USAF and VNAF. The aircraft loss data for VNAF aircraft was kept by the HQ VNAF Office of Safety and covers the period from the beginning of 1962 to the end of July 1973. Although incomplete, the data provides a representative sample of losses throughout the Vietnam War.

Further information on the aircraft, and the men that flew it, can be found at http://skyraider.org and http://a-1combatjournal.com. These two websites have been online since 1997, and they provide a wealth of information for both historians and modellers alike.

ACKNOWLEDGEMENTS

I owe special thanks to Wayne Mutza, Warren Thompson and Robert F Dorr for allowing me access to their extensive image collections. A special thank you to William Reeder who shared his story of experiences as a POW in Vietnam. Special thanks to Chris Hobson, author of *Vietnam Air Losses*, for making his work available to the A-1 Skyraider Association in its entirety. Also thanks to the following individuals who shared images and/or Skyraider stories with me – Jake Ludwig, Bill Stevens, Tom Bigelow, Herb Tidwell, Rob Cole, Richard Keogh, Don Wilkerson, Peter Bird, Andy Renshaw, Mike Roberts and William H Mogan. USAF Skyraider pilots who shared stories and images were Don Emigholz, Joe Saueressig, Herb Meyr, Dick Foreman, Ed Homan, Jim Partington, Don Engebretsen, Charlie Holder, Randy Scott, Gary Koldyke, Larry Haight, Jim Madden, John Larrison, Win DePoorter, Tom Dwelle, Dick Allen, John Lackey (via Roy Lackey), Mike Maloney, Alan Young, Davis Glass, Shelley Hilliard, Bill Prescott, 'Jink' Bender and Ron Smith.

I am indebted to the following VNAF Skyraider pilots who shared images and stories – Nguyen Quoc Dat, Pham Minh Xuan, Ho Van Hien, Nguyen Tranh Trung, Duong Thieu Chi, Nguyen Dinh Xuan, Nguyen Chuyen, Nguyen Quoc Thanh, Hoi B Tran, Thai Ngoc Truong Van, Nguyen Lanh and Son Bach. I sincerely apologise to those who assisted me but are not listed here. Your help was greatly appreciated.

SKYRAIDER AND ITS ORDNANCE

The Skyraider is a single-engined attack aircraft of low-wing monoplane design with conventional retractable landing gear. First operational with the US Navy in 1945, Skyraider production ended in 1957 when the final AD-7 (the 3180th Skyraider built by Douglas Aircraft) rolled off the production line. Recommended maximum gross weight was 25,000 lbs. This included 8000 lbs of external ordnance/fuel on 15 external stations and 800 rounds of 20 mm cannon ammunition.

The aircraft is powered by a Wright Cyclone 18 R-3350-26WA with a single-stage, two-speed supercharger. It is an 18-cylinder, two-row, air-cooled, radial engine, rated at 2700 horsepower at takeoff – it also produces great amounts of torque. Part of the unique design of this engine was that it was built using a dry sump lubrication system to lubricate almost all engine components, versus internal lubrication paths. Consequently, there was always a lot of oil in and around the engine, given its 38.5-gallon engine sump – so much in fact that it was normally dripping out the bottom of the engine cowl onto other parts of the aircraft.

There was a saying that you could always pick out a Skyraider pilot in a crowd, as he was the one with the larger right leg developed from his constant need to use right rudder thanks to the engine torque. He would also be wearing a dirty, oily, flightsuit! If you were a maintenance man and worked on a Skyraider, you were never able to approach the A-1 without getting oil on something. Many were known to keep an extra set of fatigues in a locker that they donned whenever they went out to the flightline to work on the A-1.

The design, development and production of the AD Skyraider have been well documented in previous publications, and are beyond the scope of this book. Instead, I will focus on the four models of Skyraider that saw service with the USAF and VNAF. All the A-1s used by these two air forces during the Vietnam War had initially served with the US Navy, and some had seen action flying from carrier decks earlier in the Vietnam War (see *Osprey Combat Aircraft 77 – US Navy A-1 Skyraider Units of the Vietnam War* for further details).

On 18 September 1962, the United States introduced the Tri-Service aircraft designation system that changed the designation for all military aircraft. In the case of the Skyraider, these designation changes were as follows – AD-5 to A-1E, AD-5N to A-1G, AD-5Q to EA-1F, AD-5W to EA-1E, AD-6 to A-1H and AD-7 to A-1J.

All A-1 Skyraiders had six-digit serials that were actually Bureau Numbers (BuNos) assigned by the US Navy's Bureau of Aeronautics when the aircraft

Delivered to the VNAF in May 1961, AD-6 135228 bears the markings of the 1st FS at Bien Hoa. Loaded with four rocket pods, six M1A frag clusters and four napalm tanks, this Skyraider is ideally loaded for a CAS mission. The lack of an external fuel tank is testament to both the close proximity of targets to Bien Hoa and the low fuel consumption of the Skyraider (*USAF*)

was first ordered from Douglas. This unique six-digit number for each Skyraider identified it for the rest of its life. A-1s that went to the VNAF directly from the US Navy retained this six-digit number, which was displayed on the aircraft as part of its national markings.

The USAF, however, already had its own serial number system for its aircraft. Wisely, the six-digit BuNo for each of the Skyraiders it acquired was retained, preceded by the last two digits of the fiscal year in which the aircraft was ordered for production. Since the oldest USAF Skyraiders (and the first procured) were A-1Es (formerly AD-5s) that were ordered in 1952, the 52 prefix followed by a hyphen became the aircrafts' USAF serial number. For example, A-1E BuNo 132643 became 52-132643.

USAF records indicate that there was an abortive attempt in 1968 to assign 53, 54 and 55 as prefixes to newer model Skyraiders as they were acquired by the USAF, but later in that same year the records show that the prefixes were all changed back to 52. This means that all USAF Skyraiders, no matter the model, were assigned a 52 prefix. For this book, all references to specific Skyraiders will cite only the six-digit BuNo, referring to it as a serial number.

VNAF SKYRAIDERS

The VNAF was provided with 25 AD-6 Skyraiders in 1960 to replace its ageing F8F Bearcats through the Military Assistance Program. The first of these aircraft arrived in Saigon on 24 September 1960, and after processing and flight testing they were flown from Tan Son Nhut AB to Bien Hoa AB to enter service with the VNAF. Over the next six years, further deliveries added a sufficient number of A-1s to allow the equipment of four additional squadrons. By January 1966 the VNAF had 146 Skyraiders assigned to it.

As far as is known, the only modifications made to Skyraiders transferred to the VNAF from the US Navy were the removal of all equipment associated with the delivery of nuclear weapons and the tailhook. The earliest A-1H Skyraiders even kept the US Navy paint scheme, but with US markings replaced by those of the VNAF. In one of the many ironies of the Vietnam War, the first USAF A-1Es based at Bien Hoa bore VNAF markings from June 1964 until February 1965 in an effort to mask the presence of American combat aircraft in South Vietnam. Many photographs exist of these early USAF Skyraiders incorrectly identified as belonging to the VNAF in various books, magazines and journals.

A significant change to the appearance of VNAF Skyraiders (and all their aircraft for that matter) occurred with the introduction of camouflage paint in 1966. From the very start, VNAF Skyraider markings had been flamboyant and eye-catching, and the addition of camouflage did not change this. During this period A-1s exhibited a mixture of flamboyance and stealth – a seeming contradictory combination for a combat aircraft. However, during the later stages of the war, VNAF Skyraiders were much more subdued in their overall appearance.

In 1967, Stanley Aviation Corporation's Yankee Extraction System was installed in all VNAF Skyraiders. This system functioned by means of an extraction rocket similar in principle to the drogue gun system on a normal ejection seat. Once the catapult charge fired, the spin-stabilised rocket was fired when the pendant lines reached full stretch. Actuation of the system was effected after the canopy had been jettisoned. The rocket was then erected by means of a pyrotechnic piston and lever under the erector/launcher. The rocket launched from the rear wall of the cockpit, and by means of a pair of Perlon pendants (rope-like straps), the pilot was pulled up and out of the cockpit. His parachute was rigged with an automatic opening system which activated after the rocket pendants separated from the parachute risers. The system included a set of rails to allow the seat back to rise up, while the seat pan was articulated to assist in the positioning of the pilot to the vertical as the rocket extracted him from the cockpit.

Shown flying over the Eglin AFB ranges, A-1E 132417 was one of two Skyraiders evaluated by the USAF for use in Counter Insurgency (COIN) Warfare in 1962-63. Looking suspiciously clean for a Skyraider, this aircraft must have been photographed very soon after it had been repainted in USAF markings. This early scheme gave way to one that saw more black paint applied further aft on the forward fuselage where oil and exhaust stains typically built up (*USAF via Hukee collection*)

By the late 1960s losses and ongoing conversion of some VNAF A-1 units to the A-37 Dragonfly meant that there were just 69 operational Skyraiders available to oppose the surprise communist Tet Offensive of January 1968. USAF Skyraiders began to be transferred to the VNAF through MAP at around this time too, these aircraft being configured slightly differently to the Skyraiders procured directly from the US Navy – the USAF A-1s were still fitted with tailhooks, for example.

In total, the VNAF operated 329 Skyraiders, of which 240 came from the US Navy and the remaining 89 from the USAF as MAP transfers (most of the latter were supplied between 1970 and 1972). According to one account, the VNAF lost a total of 242 Skyraiders either in combat or to non-combat related accidents. However, it could be said that in the end all the Skyraiders supplied to the VNAF were lost since the air force ceased to exist following the fall of Saigon at the end of April 1975.

USAF SKYRAIDERS

If you thought that USAF Skyraiders were the same as US Navy Skyraiders except for their exterior colour schemes, you would be wrong. Two A-1Es on loan from the US Navy (BuNos 132417 and 132439) were evaluated by Tactical Air Command's Special Air Warfare Center (SAWC) at Eglin AFB, Florida, from August 1962 to January 1963. The stated purpose of the test was to 'evaluate the A-1E Skyraider for possible use in counterinsurgency warfare, and gauge its maintenance supportability and requirements'.

The conclusions reached were that the A-1E was an aircraft in the operational inventory that could perform many roles peculiar to counterinsurgency warfare, and after completion of minor modifications it would be capable of carrying all conventional ordnance of the 2000-lb or smaller class either then in the inventory or programmed for production.

The following items required modification or new installation:

1. Newest version R-3350 engine (R-3350-26WD)
2. Landing and taxi lights
3. Parking brake
4. Speed-brake well doors (never implemented)
5. N-9 gun camera to replace installed N-6 camera
6. Dual controls to include rudder/wheel brakes and control column with trim controls. Engine controls were listed as not required (a requirement for a throttle was added at a later time)
7. The right-hand side of the glare shield required modification to prevent the blocking of important warning lights from view
8. A pneumatic tailwheel to replace the existing hard solid rubber wheel to allow operations on a variety of runway and parking ramp surfaces.
9. Exterior paint and markings consistent with applicable USAF regulations
10. Aircraft technical order revisions to reflect modifications made

Although these modifications were based solely on the testing of the A-1E aircraft in 1962-63, many of them applied to the other models of Skyraider that would be procured in the future.

The first aircraft delivered to the USAF were A-1Es in mid-1964. After numerous programme changes regarding the distribution of these first machines, 25 went to Tactical Air Command (TAC) to be used for Skyraider upgrade training at Hurlburt Field, Florida. A further 48 USAF A-1Es were at Bien Hoa AB by the end of 1964, by which point eight Skyraiders had been lost with the death of six American pilots and two Vietnamese observers.

In mid-1967 the USAF was able to acquire single-seat A-1H/Js from the US Navy, and these aircraft underwent a similar modification programme to that undertaken with the A-1E, except of course for the changes relating to the second set of flight controls – H- and J-models were single-seat Skyraiders. Once completed, the aircraft were transported by ship to Southeast Asia, arriving at their respective units about a month after the modifications had been completed. These deliveries began in late 1967, and were largely complete by the end of 1968.

The A-1E was a multipurpose version of the Skyraider developed to permit greater versatility either as an attack aircraft or in the utility role. It departed from previous variants in that it had side-by-side seating for two crewmembers. The A-1E was powered by the R-3350-26WA engine and fully equipped to carry bombs, rockets, torpedoes, mines and other stores on external racks. Four M3 20 mm cannons were installed in the wings. The aircraft could also be equipped with auxiliary tanks both internally and externally for long-range operations. For utility purposes, the aircraft could quickly be equipped with seating for passengers, as well as facilities for the carriage of litter patients or provisions.

USAF A-1Es were produced from four different US Navy variants, namely the AD-5, AD-5N, AD-5Q and AD-5W. These A-1Es subsequently proved to be the mainstay of the first group of Skyraiders used by the USAF and, later, by the VNAF. Gone were the bulbous radomes and electronics pods carried on the inner stations of the AD-5Q/W, as well as the opaque rear canopies with a single viewing port on each side. The latter were eventually replaced with the blue plastic enclosures that gave rise to the nickname 'blue room' for the space behind the two front side-by-side seats of the USAF's A-1Es.

A close variant of the A-1E was the A-1E-5, which differed from the USAF's standard E-model through its lack of right-seat controls. In order to expedite the delivery of additional A-1Es to Southeast Asia in the 1965-66 timeframe, the installation of right seat controls for these aircraft was not accomplished. By mid-1966 the training of VNAF pilots by USAF units in Southeast Asia had ended, thus removing the need for dual-control A-1Es. However, no E-5s were sent to the 'Skyraider school' at Hurlburt AFB, in Florida, for obvious reasons. Other than by looking at the tail number, there was no easy way an observer could tell the difference between an A-1E and an A-1E-5 from the outside. It would be a gross understatement to say that no self-respecting Skyraider pilot wanted to be in the right seat of an A-1E-5 in combat!

There were three A-1E-5s assigned to the 1st Special Operations Squadron (SOS) when I arrived at Nakhon Phanom (NKP) Royal Thai Air Force Base (RTAFB) in October 1971, and I flew ('rode!') in the right seat of one three times, hating every minute of it. There was a check-out programme in the 1st SOS at this time that required all new pilots to first ride in the right seat of the E or E-5, then get in the left seat for a few more flights with an IP (instructor pilot), before going solo in either the E-, H- or J-model Skyraider. The IPs in our squadron hated to be in the right seat of the E-5, but there they were.

The USAF's A-1G closely resembled the E-model, being formerly designated the AD-5N in US Navy service. This aircraft was designed as the three-seat night-attack variant of the AD-5, and for all intents and purposes the A-1G was different from the E-model only in ways we pilots could not detect. Without looking up the serial number or searching through the aircraft's maintenance paperwork, there really was no way of telling a USAF A-1E from an A-1G.

Because of what became termed the 'USAF A-1E standard', many US Navy-designated A-1Gs became Air Force A-1Es. A 'standard A-1E' was produced when all the USAF-stipulated modifications had been made prior to an aircraft seeing frontline service. Some A-1Gs were only partially modified due their urgent requirement as attrition replacements in Southeast Asia, which in turn meant that they kept their US Navy designations.

GUN PROBLEMS

Several problem areas afflicted both USAF and VNAF A-1s in frontline service in Southeast Asia. Probably the most important of these was the reliability of the wing-mounted M3 20 mm guns, which posed a problem throughout the aircraft's service life. The guns used old Korean War-vintage percussion-primed 20 mm ammunition. There were many instances of jammed guns, or worse, exploding guns resulting from a double feed or premature detonation of the round.

Additionally, there were instances where extremely long-firing bursts could lead to overheating and subsequent premature detonations. Our experience

near the end of the USAF Skyraider's time in Vietnam was that we virtually never fired all four guns at once, and our bursts were kept short – less than two seconds in duration. At 12 rounds per second per gun, this was still a lethal burst. Despite these restrictions, it was still quite rare to return from a mission without at least one jammed gun.

Armament personnel examine the damage caused to an A-1 when a 20 mm round exploded in the chamber of one of the left wing-mounted M3 cannons. These kinds of problems undoubtedly led to the loss of more than a few Skyraiders in service with the USAF. The development and use of 'bore safe' ammunition helped reduce the instances of explosions due to overheated barrels or the double feeding of guns (*Larry Haight*)

In August 1965, Headquarters Pacific Air Forces made the decision to camouflage all USAF aircraft in Southeast Asia. This of course affected all Skyraiders then in-theatre, plus those undergoing modification for shipment to Southeast Asia. A goal was set to complete the camouflage of all Skyraiders in South Vietnam by the end of 1966. The result was a profound change in the appearance of all aircraft in-theatre. This camouflage scheme would become standard for all tactical combat aircraft in the USAF well into the 1980s.

As with most piston-engined aircraft designed and built prior to 1960, the Skyraider had no means for the pilot to escape should the need arise when operating at low altitudes – essentially below 2000 ft. With the A-1 typically operating well below the recommended safe bailout altitude of 2000 ft while performing its mission, the only choice available for most pilots was to crash-land the aircraft if they could. Many could not, however, and the loss rate for aircraft and pilots proved to be unacceptably high as a result.

In an effort to improve a pilot's chances of survival, the USAF contracted Stanley Aviation Corporation in 1965 to develop an automated escape system for the Skyraider. The company's answer was the extraction seat. The seat would remain in the aircraft, and the pilot would be pulled out in a standing position, attached to a rocket-propelled tether. By 20 April 1967, the task of installing the Yankee Extraction System in all USAF A-1Es in Southeast Asia had been completed.

Numerous A-1E Skyraiders line the ramp at McClellan AFB, near Sacramento, California, in 1967. The Skyraider modification schedule was accelerated to offset the heavy losses suffered by A-1 units in Southeast Asia (*USAF*)

It did not take long for the newly installed system to prove its worth, for on 21 May 1967 Maj James Holler's Skyraider (133855) of the 1st Air Commando Squadron (ACS) was hit by ground fire shortly after departing

Pleiku AB. Holler was about 1000 ft above the ground when he activated the extraction system, and although he subsequently landed on rocky ground and broke both ankles, this was the first successful use of the Yankee Extraction System. Shortly thereafter, on 11 June, Majs James Rauch and Robert Russell became the second and third satisfied customers of the Stanley Aviation product when their Skyraider (132408) experienced a loss of power during their air strike in northern Laos (possibly due to battle damage). Forced to extract about 1500 ft above the ground, both men landed safely and were rescued by a USAF Jolly Green HH-3 helicopter.

However, it should be noted that there were subsequently some problems with the Yankee system, which had many safety features that required 'man-in-the-loop' inspection and preparation. Some easy-to-miss items in the checklist were predictably overlooked, with disastrous results. Following each failure, there were modifications made to either procedures or equipment, or perhaps both. I can definitely say that by the time I flew the Skyraider in combat in 1971-72, the system was very reliable, and had the confidence of those of us who flew aircraft with it installed. There is no way of knowing how many lives could have been saved if the Yankee Extraction System had been fitted in the A-1 from the very beginning, but certainly it would have been a significant number. During my year-long tour we had six extractions and six survivors, and all concerned were rescued.

SKYRAIDER ORDNANCE

The A-1's 12 outer wing stations were able to carry 500-lb class stores. The two Inboard Stations (commonly called stubs) carried up to 2000 lbs each and the Centerline Station could cope with up to 3600 lbs of ordnance. Multiple ejector racks (MERs) could be fitted on the Inboard Stations to increase the number of munitions loaded. Ordnance carried by both USAF and VNAF Skyraiders can be grouped into the following categories – guns, bombs, napalm, rockets, cluster bombs (CBUs) and miscellaneous stores.

The four internal M3 guns carried 200 rounds of percussion-primed 20 mm ammunition each. The weapons were fired in pairs, inboards or outboards. The nominal rate-of-fire was 600-800 rounds per minute (10-14 rounds per second), which meant guns could be fired out in approximately ten seconds. There were two types of 20 mm rounds typically used for combat, the M95 Armor Piercing Tracer (APT) and the M97 High Explosive Incendiary (HEI). Muzzle velocity for both rounds was 2730 ft per second.

The SUU-11 gun pod (known as the minigun) was also often carried on the Inboard Station(s). This was a six-barrel Gatling-type weapon that was rated at 6000 rounds per minute (100 rounds per second). The minigun, which carried 1500 rounds of 7.62 mm ammunition, was a very effective weapon for close-in work around friendly troops or a downed aviator during a SAR mission.

This A-1E of the 34th TG is loaded with an M117 GP bomb on the left Inboard Station (stub) and M57 GP bombs on stations 4 and 6. Stations 1 (just out of shot to right), 2, 3 and 5 are loaded with M1A frag clusters. It would be correct to assume that a load identical to this would also be hung beneath the aircraft's right wing. Note the early version 'Daisy Cutter" extenders on the GP bombs. Bore plugs cover the muzzles of the M3 cannons (*John Larrison*)

The A-1 carried three main types of bombs – general-purpose (GP) bombs, fragmentation bombs and white phosphorus bombs (WP).

The earliest GP bombs used by A-1s were those left over from Korean War stockpiles that in fact originated from World War 2. These were available in a variety of sizes, and could be used with either box or conical fins. The designations for the bombs that were most often carried on the A-1 were M30 (100-lb), M57 (250-lb), M64 (500-lb), M117 (750-lb) and M66 (1000-lb).

These older GP bombs of lower yield were very good for supporting friendly troops under close attack by enemy forces. They could be dropped within 100 ft of protected friendly troops against enemy forces in the open. Indeed, it was this type of weapon that Skyraider crews used when helping to defend the besieged Special Forces Camp in the A Shau Valley in early 1966, with Maj Bernie Fisher carrying ten M30 100-lb GP bombs and two M47 100-lb white phosphorous bombs on his A-1 during his Medal of Honor mission on 10 March.

An improved family of GP bombs (referred to as low drag GP or LDGP) was developed by the US Navy in the late 1960s. Designated the Mark (Mk) 8X series, these were a big improvement over earlier GP bombs. The sizes available were Mk 81 (250-lb), Mk 82 (500-lb), Mk 83 (1000-lb) and Mk 84 (2000-lb).

All GP bombs required fuses – typically a nose and tail fuse for redundancy. The fuse was a timer that armed the weapon after it had fallen for a predetermined period following its release, allowing the aircraft to be safely away from the blast. Fuse extenders (referred to as 'Daisy Cutters') were often used to ensure that the bomb detonated before penetrating soft earth. The Skyraider pilots of the 1st ACS and 602nd Fighter Squadron (Commando), pioneered the early use of 'Daisy Cutters'. Initially, a non-serviceable 20 mm gun barrel was welded to the bomb nose plug that was then threaded back into the fuse well of the bomb. Later, an iron pipe was welded to the fuse plug instead. The problem with the extenders was that they were often not aligned to the longitudinal axis of the bomb, which resulted in diminished accuracy.

These early efforts got the attention of the munitions professionals, and before too long production fuse extenders were used not just by A-1s, but also by the entire force of both fighters and bombers from all services in Southeast Asia.

A-1E 134990 cruises above the undercast towards its target in early 1966. The ordnance load of 12 M57 GP and two M47 WP bombs, plus the 300-gallon Centerline tank, would have put the aircraft's gross weight for takeoff at a little under 20,000 lbs. This A-1E was lost in combat on 9 April 1969 during a *Barrel Roll* mission at night, the pilot of the 22nd SOS machine, Maj R H Shumock, being rescued. The loss report stated that the A-1 was hit by groundfire on Shumock's ninth pass – apparently one pass too many (*Richard E Allen Collection*)

Early fragmentation bombs were used when enemy troops were the expected target. M81 and M88 fragmentation bombs were 250-lb class weapons that were essentially the same bar their slightly different construction. Their similarity allowed them to be fielded interchangeably. A more commonly used fragmentation bomb was the M1A frag cluster bomb. It consisted of a pre-built cluster of six 20-lb fragmentation bomblets banded together in a six-bomb cluster. The M1A was used throughout the war by A-1s of both services.

The final member of the bomb family was the M47 100-lb WP weapon. The favoured munition of many USAF A-1 pilots, it was used in the early stages of the conflict, as well as at the very end. The bomb's white phosphorus filler, which burned at a higher temperature than napalm, spread on impact when the weapon was dropped armed. If dropped safe, the bomb would crack open on ground contact and the white phosphorus would provide a smoke marker visible from the air for more than an hour.

Napalm was often used, being expended in 500- and 750-lb versions. The smaller of these two was carried on the outer wing stations of the A-1, whilst the larger could only be carried on the Inboard Stations. Early napalm stores were mixed and loaded on base, but later versions were premixed off base and supplied to units ready to load. Once the weapon was attached to an aircraft, installation of the fuse was all that remained. Napalm came in finned and unfinned versions. Finned 'nape' allowed for better accuracy, but limited the weapon's 'splash' pattern. Since the Skyraider was very accurate due to its low speed, unfinned napalm was preferred due to its wider burn pattern.

The A-1 also regularly used rockets, of which there were two different kinds (irrespective of the warhead) compatible with the aircraft. More common was the 2.75-in FFAR (Folding Fin Aerial Rocket), which was always carried in a launcher pod of either seven or 19 tubes. The seven-tube rocket pods were the LAU-59 and LAU-68, while the 19-tube pods were the LAU-19 and LAU-3. Rockets could be fired singly in the seven-tube launcher, but had to be fired in pairs (all bar the first rocket, which was a single shot) out of the 19-tube launchers.

Warheads for the 2.75-in FFARs could be white phosphorus (WP or 'Willy Pete'), high explosive (HE), high-explosive anti-tank (HEAT) or flechette. The latter warhead contained approximately 2500 stamped darts that look like six-penny finishing nails with three circular shaped fins instead of a nail head. Normally, an entire pod would be loaded with a single type of warhead, rather than having them mixed.

The other, less common, type of rocket was the 5-in high velocity aerial rocket (HVAR), which was single-mounted to the outer wing station pylons. Thus, a maximum load of 12 could be carried on one sortie.

This A-1 is loaded with 12 M47 WP bombs and two CBU-30 dispensers, this specialised load being used for SAR missions when 'area denial' – denying the enemy access to a survivor – was the priority. The M47 bombs were used to provide a wall of smoke to shield the SAR helicopter from enemy firing positions. The CBU-30 contained CS gas that was a non-lethal incapacitant used when the enemy was too close to the survivor for the employment of lethal weapons (*John Lackey via Roy Lackey*)

The cluster bomb units (CBUs) dropped from Skyraiders were different from those used by jet aircraft of the period. In 1964, William M Mogan and his team at the First Combat Applications Group at Hurlburt Field developed a new CBU dispenser specifically for the A-1, the SUU-14. Just over six feet in length, it consisted of six tubes arranged in a triangular shape held together by reinforcing metal. What was different with this dispenser was that it stayed attached to the A-1 and the bomblets were ejected out the back of it.

According to Mogan, 'the concept of the SUU-14 dispenser evolved at a dinner in Fort Walton Beach one night between USAF types and a designer for Aerojet General. The idea of the SUU-14 was generated from the need to get bomblets out of a tube in a dispenser that was flying at the slow speeds of the A-1E. It was drawn up on a napkin and a prototype was cobbled together.

'The idea was simple – a small gas generator was used to push bomblets out of the rear of the tube. It you chose "ripple", the intervalometer allowed the pilot to dial in a speed [in milliseconds], after which a single push of the firing button would empty all six tubes sequentially. The resulting pattern took the form of a continuous string on the ground. If you went manually [singles], you could drop six smaller strings, or one string per pass.

'I did some good work on the SUU-14, going a month virtually without sleep so as to get a contract placed for the dispenser that would allow it to go into production. It was the first modern item tailored for the A-1. The SUU-14 dispenser duly allowed the highly accurate delivery of cluster sub-munitions.'

The first CBU munition to use the SUU-14 dispenser was the CBU-14, which worked fine against targets in the open but was inadequate in forested areas because the BLU-3 bomblet would detonate in the treetops, which may have been 100 ft or more above the enemy. Additionally, the dud rate for the BLU-3 was quite high, and provided the enemy with a supply of anti-personnel munitions for use against friendly troops in the form of booby traps.

Recognising the need for an improved CBU munition for the Skyraider, a second version was developed and fielded in September 1970. Still using the innovative SUU-14 dispenser, the CBU-25 contained 132 BLU-24

A-1E 132659 is seen here loaded with ten SUU-14 dispensers and two 750-lb napalm tanks on the inboard stations. The 300-gallon Centerline tank could carry up to 2000 lbs of fuel. A groundcrewman would remove the red safety streamers prior to takeoff (*Tom Dwelle*)

bomblets (22 per tube) with fusing that allowed them to penetrate the jungle canopy before they detonated. The CBU-25 proved to be a great improvement over its predecessor, the CBU-14. Indeed, it was used on nearly every load we carried during my tour, and was featured on the 'Sandy' mission load.

Another CBU that used the SUU-14 dispenser was the CBU-22, which contained 72 BLU-17 white phosphorus smoke bomblets. The CBU-22 was used as an incendiary weapon, or to create a dense smoke screen to shield rescue helicopters from an enemy ground threat.

An interesting munition that was used when Skyraiders were in the 'truck killing' role over the Ho Chi Minh Trail was the M36 incendiary bomb, referred to by A-1 pilots who employed the weapon as the 'funny bomb'. The M36 was developed during World War 2, which in fact it helped bring to an end. The bomb was one of the principal weapons used in the fire-bombing of Japanese cities that quickly led to the dropping of the atomic bomb and the surrender of Japan. Somewhere, somehow, stocks of these leftover munitions were located and shipped to Nakhon Phanom for use by A-26s and A-1s, which were the principal truck killers on the trail in 1969.

Although the M36 functioned much like a more modern CBU, technically it was not a CBU. Rather than bomblets being ejected from a dispenser, with the M36 its bomb casing split open and dispensed thermite grenades that consumed anything with which they came into contact, including trucks. It was the weapon of choice, with the grenades putting on quite a pyrotechnics show since the M36 was almost exclusively used at night. For that same reason very few photographs exist of this weapon.

This A-1 from the 22nd SOS boasts the quintessential ordnance load for killing trucks on the Ho Chi Minh Trail. The M36 incendiary bomb, better known as the 'funny bomb' to the pilots who carried it, was perhaps the best weapon available for this mission. Once released, the clamshell canister split open, dispensing 182 thermite bomblets that ignited anything they contacted. The rocket pod contains rounds fitted with either anti-personnel flechette or WP warheads. Napalm, M1A frag clusters and flares round out the load (*Mike Maloney*)

The Madden Kit contained survival-related items that a downed airman might need to facilitate his rescue (*Alan Young*)

Anti-personnel area denial munitions were occasionally used to prevent an approaching enemy from directly contacting friendly forces on the ground. These munitions were chemical (non-lethal) riot control agents that would incapacitate personnel for varying periods of time ranging from 15 minutes to two hours. This category of munition was not used by the VNAF.

These weapons could be delivered in two main ways by the A-1. The BLU-52 was actually a 750-lb napalm tank filled with CS agent in powderised form. No fuse was needed when employing this munition because the thin-walled case of the tank ruptured on impact with the ground, dispensing its powder over a wide area.

The CBU-19 and CBU-30 could also be used in conjunction with non-lethal CS agent, the latter being contained within small bomblets that were in turn packed into the CBU canister. The CBU dispensers were retained on the aircraft, with their contents being ejected out the bottom of the canisters. This method of delivery covered a wider area than the BLU-52. The CBU-19 was used in the early war years, before being replaced by the improved CBU-30.

One final store that was available to drop was the Madden Kit. This was not a weapon but rather a 'survival kit' that contained items – maps, a survival radio and/or batteries, signalling devices, water or food – that a downed airman needed to facilitate his rescue.

In February 1971, Lt Jim Madden was 'Sandy Low' during a SAR mission near Mu Gia Pass. After two days, the airman concerned remained unrescued, and the batteries for his survival radio were depleted. Madden thought there must be a way to get batteries to a survivor. Being his squadron's Life Support officer, he checked with his Life Support NCOs and soon found out that no container existed of which they were aware for battery dispensing from the air.

After a brainstorming session, one of the NCOs suggested an empty flare canister. After a few failed attempts at fabricating a device that could hold the requited items, testing was done with the support of the wing commander. Madden soon had a Skyraider at his disposal, and various versions were loaded for testing. The store that was chosen was a kit with high drag fins that would slow the canister down before impact. It was painted bright yellow so that it would be easy to spot among the green vegetation of the jungle. This version of the canister was available for us to drop when I was a 'Sandy' at Nakhon Phanom later that same year. The Madden Kit canister was not automatically loaded for each and every mission, but it was quickly available should one have been needed.

ORIGINAL SKYRAIDER UNITS

The history of the first VNAF fighter unit, appropriately designated the 1st Fighter Squadron (FS), begins on 1 June 1956 when it received 22 cast-off F8F Bearcats from the French *Armée de l'Air*. However, the unit's association with the Skyraider commenced on 23 September 1960 with the arrival of its first six former US Navy AD-6s – just five short years after the formal beginning of the Air Force of South Vietnam. The VNAF desperately wanted to upgrade its capability so that it could support the Army of the Republic of Vietnam (ARVN) in its struggle with the Viet Cong (VC), which was growing in both numbers and effectiveness. With the arrival of the Skyraider, that capability became reality. A further 19 AD-6s reached Vietnam in increments, until all 25 aeroplanes of the 1st FS had arrived by the end of May 1961.

The first group of VNAF Skyraider pilots received their conversion training from US Navy instructors at Naval Air Station (NAS) Corpus Christi, Texas. These first A-1 pilots were a capable group that had originally been trained by the French and had already seen combat in the T-28 and/or F8F Bearcat. One former US Navy Skyraider instructor recalled, 'I remember that we (the instructors) felt that the Vietnamese were at a big disadvantage because of their lack of experience with machinery in general, and because of the language problems that they encountered. But I laugh when I think about how we "Hot Shot Naval Aviators" would have made out in a flying school in Vietnam'.

Lt Col Nguyen Quoc Thanh was one of the early VNAF pilots to be trained at NAS Corpus Christi;

'Oh it was a big aeroplane! I didn't realise how big it was until I walked up to it and stood next to the prop and looked up at the huge engine.

'There were no two-seat AD-5s available for us to make our first Skyraider flights, so I was scared. Five of us students all took off at

This static display of A-1H 135228 at Bien Hoa shows the vast array of weapons that could be carried by the Skyraider. Just forward of the aircraft's engine is a Mk 8 300-gallon Centerline fuel tank, distinguishable by the centre seam that ran horizontally around it. Two 20 mm M3 cannons are displayed, along with 20 mm ammunition links that are arranged to show '514' – this aircraft was clearly assigned to the 514th FS, formerly designated the 1st FS until 17 June 1963 (*Joe Saueressig*)

Two A-1Hs with folded wings return from a mission in 1964. Note the Satan markings contained within a diagonal band just forward of the tail of A-1H 135256. The aircraft's cocked tailwheel indicates that the A-1 has manoeuvered to the right side of the taxiway in order to avoid oncoming traffic (*Don Emigholz*)

Another view of the 'Satan' Skyraider 135256 from the 514th FS at Bien Hoa AB. Visible beneath the horizontal tail is the aircraft designation 'AD-6' (the previous identity of this particular model of Skyraider during its US Navy service) just above its BuNo. The 'Satan' motif was displayed on aircraft assigned to one of the 514th FS flights (*Don Emigholz*)

about the same time for our first flights. There were four US Navy instructors who took off first and waited for us. We took off one after the other and tried to form up in the air. The instructors were trying to find us, but it took a while for us to get together. I was so excited and nervous I forgot to close my cowl flaps. Finally, we all joined up and headed back to the field for landing. I made a very bad landing. Thinking about this flight after completing 15 years of combat in the aircraft would bring a smile to my face.'

Nguyen also recalled that for gunnery training the VNAF pilots and their instructors initially deployed to Marine Corps Air Station Yuma, Arizona, and later to NAS North Island, California. When Nguyen and his fellow aviators returned from their Skyraider training in the USA, they had ten pilots qualified to fly the A-1 and more than 20 Skyraiders on strength.

In one of the more dubious acts of the entire war, on 27 February 1962 two Skyraiders from the 1st FS took off from Bien Hoa to strike a target in the Mekong Delta region well south of Saigon. However, shortly after takeoff, 1Lt Pham Phu Quoc and his wingman 2Lt Nguyen Van Cu abruptly altered course and headed towards Saigon. Their target was the presidential palace of Ngo Dinh Diem, which they duly damaged. The president of South Vietnam escaped death. 1Lt Pham Phu Quoc was downed by AAA in Saigon and crash-landed in the Saigon River, from where he was captured and taken prisoner. 2Lt Nguyen Van Cu flew his Skyraider to Cambodia, where he sought and received political asylum.

On 1 November 1963, ARVN generals launched a *coup d'état* and succeeded in overthrowing Ngo Dinh Diem's regime. The new leadership of the VNAF released Pham and made him a squadron commander in the VNAF. Revered as a hero within the VNAF, Pham Phu Quoc was subsequently shot down and killed during a raid near Dong Hoi, in North Vietnam, in 1965. In his book *Buddah's Child*, fellow A-1 pilot and former prime minister of South Vietnam Nguyen Cao Ky said that he cried for a long time after hearing of Pham's death. Similarly restored

21

to grace, Nguyen Van Cu returned to South Vietnam from exile in Cambodia and entered politics. He was elected to the constitutional assembly and later became a congressman.

In 1965 the 514th FS was among the first VNAF units to be awarded a US Presidential Unit Citation, the squadron being 'cited for extraordinary heroism and outstanding performance of duty in combat against an armed enemy of the Republic of Vietnam throughout the period 1 January 1964 to 28 February 1965. The fierce determination to destroy the enemy displayed by the men of this unit was exemplified in the 6000 sorties and 13,000 flying hours compiled in support of ground operations during this period'. The award was signed by President Lyndon B Johnson on 26 April 1965.

The 514th would remain in the thick of the action throughout the conflict in Vietnam, resulting in the loss of 53 aircaft and 32 aircrew between 1962 and the middle of 1973. There were 14 aircraft lost in 1972 and during the first six months of 1973 alone, and it would be reasonable to assume that similar, if not greater, losses occurred in the final two years of the war.

One of the 514th pilots downed in 1972 was Capt Ho Van Hien, whose Skyraider was hit by an SA-7 shoulder-launched surface-to-air missile on 12 November near An Loc. Although he successfully used the Yankee Extraction System, his ordeal was far from over. As he was floating down beneath his parachute, enemy forces shot him in the right elbow. Despite being in a great deal of pain, Ho was able to free himself from his parachute upon landing and find cover in the undergrowth.

He soon heard enemy forces moving towards him shouting for him to surrender. Ho burrowed even deeper into the grass in an effort to remain undetected. The searchers continued to shout that they could see him, and if he surrendered they would not shoot. He knew they were bluffing as they began indiscriminately shooting into the grass. He winced but made no sound as he felt a sharp pain in his right shin, just above the ankle – he had been shot again. But they had not seen him and (*text continues on page 33*)

Two A-1Hs from the 514th FS fly in close formation near Bien Hoa AB prior to landing. Both wear the black and yellow chequerboard marking of the 23rd TW (*Jan Holley via Warren Thompson*)

1
A-1E 132637 of the 602nd FS(C), Bien Hoa AB, Republic of Vietnam, 1964

2
A-1H 135256 of the 514th, Bien Hoa AB, Republic of Vietnam, September 1964

3
A-1E 133914 of the 602nd FS(C), Bien Hoa AB, Republic of Vietnam, 1965

4
A-1H 134610 of the 83rd SAG, Bien Hoa AB, Republic of Vietnam, 1966

5
A-1H 135281 of the 518th FS, Bien Hoa AB, Republic of Vietnam, 1965

6
A-1H 137569 of the 520th FS, Binh Thuy AB, Republic of Vietnam, 1966

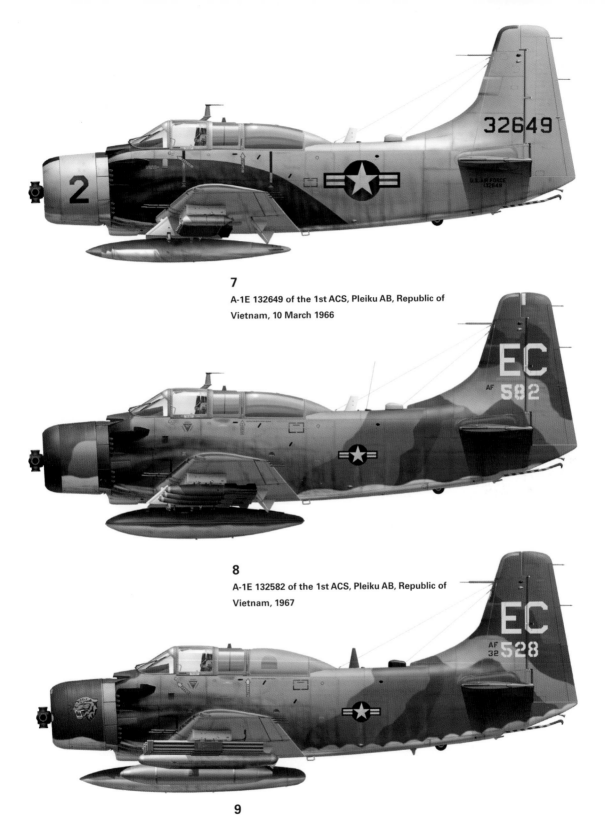

7
A-1E 132649 of the 1st ACS, Pleiku AB, Republic of
Vietnam, 10 March 1966

8
A-1E 132582 of the 1st ACS, Pleiku AB, Republic of
Vietnam, 1967

9
A-1G 132528 of the 1st ACS, Pleiku AB, Republic of Vietnam, 1967

10
A-1H 137564 of the 524th FS, Nha Trang AB, Republic of Vietnam, 1966

11
A-1E 132444 of the 602nd FS(C), Udorn RTAFB, Thailand, 11 November 1967

12
A-1E-5 135211 of the 602nd FS(C), Nakhon Phanom RTAFB, Thailand, 1968

13
A-1H 134609 of the 6th ACS, Pleiku AB, Republic of Vietnam, 1967

14
A-H 134520 of the 6th SOS, Pleiku AB, Republic of Vietnam, 1968

15
A-1H 139802 of the 516th FS, Da Nang AB, Republic of Vietnam, 1966

16

A-1H 139608 of the 1st SOS, Nakhon Phanom RTAFB, Thailand, 1968

17

A-1H 137570 of the 524th FS, Nha Trang AB, Republic of Vietnam, 1968-69

18

A-1J 142056 of the 602nd SOS, Nakhon Phanom RTAFB, Thailand, 1969

19
A-1E 133878 of the 22nd SOS, Nakhon Phanom RTAFB, Thailand, 1968-70

20
A-1H 134488 of the 516th FS, Da Nang AB, Republic of Vietnam, 1970

21
A-1E 132686 of the 4407th CCTS, Hurlburt Field, Florida, 1968

22

A-1J 142014 of the 530th FS, Pleiku AB, Republic of Vietnam, 1971

23

A-1H 137628 of the 22nd SOS, Da Nang AB, Republic of Vietnam, December 1969

24

A-1J 142072 of the 56th SOW, Nakhon Phanom RTAFB, Thailand, 1971

25
A-1E 133892 of the 514th FS, Bien Hoa AB, Republic of Vietnam, 1972

26
A-1G 133865 of the 1st SOS, Nakhon Phanom RTAFB, Thailand, 1972

27
A-1H 135332 of the 4407th CCTS, Hurlburt Field, Florida, 1971

28
A-1H 135340 of the 514th FS, Bien Hoa AB, Republic of Vietnam, 1971

29
A-1H 139665 of the 1st SOS, Nakhon Phanom RTAFB, Thailand, 1972

30
A-1H 139738 of the 1st SOS, Nakhon Phanom RTAFB, Thailand, 1972

A-1H 139703 of the 514th FS sits on the ramp at Bien Hoa on 14 December 1970 loaded with six Mk 82 GP bombs and two M117 GP bombs. The gross weight of this Skyraider as loaded is approximately 16,500 lbs, which is about 8500 lbs below its maximum gross weight. Ordnance rationing had reduced the loading of VNAF A-1s by this time, and things would get much worse for Skyraider units later in the war (*Norm Taylor via Robert F Dorr*)

he remained quiet. After about 45 minutes all was quiet. The bleeding from his elbow and leg had lessened, but Ho knew he had already lost a considerable amount of blood, and that he needed to move further away.

The searchers had by now headed off to a different location, stalking their prey, and Ho began to move in the opposite direction. As he cautiously raised himself to look around, he heard a helicopter approaching. Ho fired a flare in the direction of the sound, and the helicopter hovered over where it had initially landed. With his radio inoperable, Ho pulled out his signal smoke canister and moved towards the sound of the approaching helicopter. Soon he saw an OH-6 heading in his direction, prompting him to 'pop his smoke' and drop it at his feet. The red-orange smoke rose around him and he began to wave his arms. Soon the OH-6 came to a stop and alit beside him, and he was literally thrown onboard by a US Army crewman. The helicopter soon reached its operating base a short distance away.

Ho's biggest surprise upon being rescued was seeing his wingman holding a parachute when he landed at the helicopter base. Ho said, 'Oh, you picked up my 'chute for me?' His wingman, Lt Vu Duc Luong, replied, 'No Captain, I was shot down too'. His A-1 had been hit moments after Ho's, and he had been rescued by ARVN forces and transported to the helicopter landing area where they now stood face-to-face! The two Skyraider pilots shared a nervous laugh and were then both flown back to Bien Hoa for medical care.

Loss records show that on 12 November A-1H 139803 and A-1H 134609 were downed in the exact location recalled by Ho. During my combat tour with the 1st SOS I had flown both of these Skyraiders, and they were among the final 19 surviving USAF A-1s transferred to the VNAF less than a month prior to their loss. Ho had been downed by an SA-7 and his wingman by AAA.

Having recovered from his wounds, Ho, who was promoted to major, remained with the 514th FS until the very end of the VNAF in April 1975;

'During the final weeks of the war a portion of my squadron deployed to Phan Rang AB on 20 April. We pilots at squadron level were too far removed from the VNAF HQ in Saigon to know the whole story on how badly the war was going for us, but we were able to help defend the base. We fought side-by-side with the A-37s of the 524th and 548th FSs, both units being based at Phan Rang.

'The missions we flew from the base provided me with the best flying of my life. I remember seeing NVA trucks full of soldiers heading for Phan Rang. I will never forget seeing them looking up at me as we attacked their columns. We were supposed to be at Phan Rang for two weeks, but we had to leave after a week because the enemy was fast approaching. During that time I flew three or four sorties per day – there were so many that I could not keep track of them. We flew day and night, losing two A-1s and one pilot.

'When we were finally ordered to evacuate Phan Rang I flew back to Bien Hoa AB with 25 people in the back of my A-1E. The groundcrew had removed a panel in the rear of the "blue room" so that they could squeeze as many people as possible into the aeroplane'. What Maj Ho did not know at this moment was that the return flight to Bien Hoa was but a rehearsal for his final two A-1E missions.

The 514th FS evacuated Bien Hoa shortly thereafter too, heading for Tan Son Nhut. It was then ordered to move further south to Bien Thuy on 29 April, Ho again flying an A-1E loaded with 25 'passengers'. Following his safe landing at Bien Thuy, Ho had his aeroplane refuelled so that he could fly one last mission. The situation was now desperate on the ground, and the order was given to evacuate South Vietnam. Ho arrived back at the aircraft and found the same people he had transported to Bien Thuy, plus a few more! His final mission, and that of many other VNAF pilots, was now underway. Several Skyraiders joined up in a loose formation for the two-hour flight to U-Tapao RTAFB, in Thailand, the aircraft being led by the senior officer from the 514th FS. Ho described the scene that greeted them upon landing;

'We were disappointed to see American soldiers with their guns levelled meeting us on the ramp. They quickly applied American "stars and bars" to cover the VNAF markings on our A-1s. They took our weapons and all of our flying gear. We were devastated. We spent a couple of days at U-Tapao, and then we were flown to Guam. There, I was reunited with my fiancée and my daughter from my first marriage. We stayed there for two days before being sent to Ft Chaffee, near Little Rock, Arkansas. There, we were matched up with our sponsors. Mine was a schoolteacher friend whom I had met in 1965 when I was first in the US. We travelled to San Antonio, Texas, and he hosted me for three weeks until we could find an apartment.'

Ho subsequently remained in Texas, where he now resides.

As enemy forces rolled toward Saigon, parts of the remaining A-1 squadrons moved south to Bien Thuy AB. Lt Thai Ngoc Van had joined his squadronmates' exodus from Bien Hoa AB to Tan Son Nhut just a few days earlier. Then on 19 April the remainder of the 514th FS was ordered to further deploy to Bien Thuy AB, where Lt Thai flew his final combat missions. As one would expect, chaos reigned during these final days. Little remained of the centralised control system for the VNAF as base after base fell to the advancing enemy. Lt Thai described the situation just prior to his final combat sortie in the Skyraider;

'In late April 1975 I deployed with part of my squadron to Bien Thuy AB in IV Corps. We flew CAS missions in the vicinity of the base, as it was now being mortar bombed by the NVA on a near-daily basis. During the early morning hours of 29 April we were attacked once again. My flight leader, Maj Dinh Van Son, and I were ordered aloft on a CAS mission a short while later to support ARVN forces that were under attack. We took off in darkness, relying on the aircrafts' landing light, since neither the taxiway nor runway lights were on due to the base being in an alert condition. Each aircraft was armed with six Mk 82s and a full load of 20 mm ammunition.

'After takeoff, Maj Son contacted "Paddy Control" for tasking and we were diverted to the capital city. Saigon was under heavy attack from the NVA, especially the Tan Son Nhut AB area.

'En route to Saigon, my flight leader contacted "Paris Control" and we were directed to contact "Tinh Long 7", an AC-119K gunship that was already airborne when the attack on Tan Son Nhut commenced. My flight leader made radio contact with "Tinh Long 7" and we learned that the gunship had been working with some other A-1 flights that had taken off from Tan Son Nhut.

'As we reached our rendezvous point east of Runway 35 at Tan Son Nhut the sun was rising, and we saw that the weather over the capital city was workable – scattered clouds, with good visibility. Columns of smoke were rising up from various parts of Saigon following indiscriminate NVA mortar attacks.

'"Tinh Long 7" briefed us on the situation, and we learned that NVA forces occupied positions in populated areas very close to Tan Son Nhut – they were poised for a ground attack on the air base. Once in Saigon, NVA forces had mixed in with civilians that were trying to escape the fighting so as to use them as shields to discourage VNAF air strikes. "Tinh Long 7" was flying above us, circling the area, and we were held high and dry until the aircraft could pinpoint the NVA positions clearly so that we could bomb them without fear of harming fleeing civilians.

'Finally, "Tinh Long 7" instructed us to bomb where the tracer rounds from his miniguns were impacting. My leader rolled in for his first pass, and I followed with my bombing run as he was pulling off target. We both then awaited corrections for our next pass, but they would never come. As we looked down, we were horrified to see "Tinh Long 7" hit, probably by an SA-7. The AC-119K caught fire, broke up and spiralled down, finally impacting the ground in a big ball of fire. Briefly stunned into silence, I then radioed my lead – he had also witnessed the tragic scene below. Watching such an event left me with such an empty feeling. No words can describe witnessing the ending of people's lives that we had just talked to seconds earlier.

'After "Tinh Long 7" went down, my leader contacted "Paris Control" with a report of the tragedy, and we were ordered to get out of the area and go into a holding pattern over the base. After a brief period, we were sent over the western part of Saigon to provide more CAS strikes where the fighting was at its fiercest. We spent quite a long time over the target area, working with ARVN troops that were trying to hold their positions against a considerably larger NVA force that was advancing on Saigon. We spent all the remaining bombs and cannon rounds before heading back to Bien Thuy AB with very little fuel remaining. We both flew straight-in approaches to landing, as we feared that our engines would quit due to fuel starvation. Maj Son and I both made it down safely, thus ending the longest, and last, mission of my combat career flying the A-1.'

A-1H 135340 of the 514th FS taxis out at Bien Hoa in 1971 with a load of six Mk 81 'Ladyfinger' 250-lb LDGP bombs and two Mk 80 500-lb LDGP bombs. The A-1's manoeuvrability improved markedly when carrying a reduced weapons load such as this, giving the pilot a better chance of survival when engaged by AAA (*Tom Bigelow*)

83rd SPECIAL AIR GROUP

The VNAF was active flying 'special' type sorties from a very early stage in its history. Infiltration and re-supply missions can be traced to a small detachment called Co Trang (White Stork) established in the late 1950s. Its primary mission was to drop members of the Vietnamese Special Forces in North Vietnam, and to re-supply them when necessary. All Co Trang missions were carried out on moonlit nights using C-47s that lacked markings. A young Maj Nguyen Cao Ky volunteered for many of these early missions and eventually rose to the top of this organisation. As previously mentioned, Ky later became commander of the VNAF, followed by prime minister and vice-president of the Republic of Vietnam.

By early 1964 the Co Trang detachment had been reorganised as Biet Doan 83 (83rd Special Air Group (SAG)), also referred to as Than Phong (Divine Wind). This change coincided with Maj Ky's promotion to the rank of colonel and appointment as commander of the entire VNAF. He concurrently served as CO of the 83rd SAG too.

The unit was reinforced during this period, equipped with eight A-1H Skyraiders, two U-6 Beavers, two Cessna U-17s and a handful of H-34 helicopters. These machines were not allocated to the 83rd SAG permanently, but were loaned to the unit on a temporary basis by other VNAF squadrons. Their arrival meant that the 83rd could now carry out a wide variety of covert missions in both North and South Vietnam.

One of the first pilots to fly A-1s with the unit in early 1964 was Maj Nguyen Quoc Thanh (who at that time was the CO of the 518th FS);

'Just after the formation of the 83rd SAG by Col Ky I was asked to report to his office. Ky said, "I've heard about you Thanh. How would you like to join Co Trong at Tan Son Nhut?" When the head of the Air Force asks if you want to work for him, of course I said I would be honoured, which I was.'

Maj Thanh explained that although the 83rd SAG Skyraiders primarily supported ARVN Special Forces in South Vietnam during his time with the unit, the aircraft were also frequently tasked with flying strikes against NVA targets. In order to reach these sites north of Dong Hoi, the A-1s were frequently deployed to Nakhon Phanom RTAFB. The 83rd normally took four A-1s at a time on these deployments, the aircraft typically being loaded with 300-gallon Centreline Tanks and either six or eight Mk 82 bombs when flying missions from the base. Maj Thanh explained that the A-1s would usually stay at Nakhon Phanom for about two weeks at a time. They always flew at night in two-ship formations, and following their strikes they would recover back to the Thai base.

For targets south of Dong Hoi, they staged out of Da Nang. It was on one such night mission that Maj Thanh ended up floating in a rubber raft. He and his wingman were striking a target near Dong Hoi, which was about 30 nautical miles north of the demilitarised zone (DMZ) that separated North

VNAF Skyraider pilots assigned to the 83rd SAG pose with their American advisors in front of one of their specially marked A-1s. Many of them are wearing their trademark black flying suits that identified them as 83rd SAG pilots. The aircraft behind them is loaded with M30 GP bombs. The marking on the engine cowl (in yellow) is Cuu Xung, which in English means 'the best of the best' (*Author's collection*)

The 'Than Phong' camouflage scheme on this A-1 preceded the Southeast Asian scheme that was introduced by the USAF in 1966 and subsequently adopted by the VNAF. 'Than Phong' used two different shades of green and darker browns than the USAF scheme. Even after the 83rd SAG had been disbanded in early 1968, the older scheme could still be seen adorning aircraft flown by various A-1 units, as the group's Skyraiders were reassigned throughout the VNAF (*Author's collection*)

A-1H 134610 of the 83rd SAG is seen here flying over open water, perhaps returning from a low-level training mission off the Vietnamese coast. The marking on the cowl is Cuu Sach, which means 'the better' in English. Note the number '83' hand-painted on the Centerline tank, which was probably applied by a crew chief who was tired of having his tanks 'stolen' at Tan Son Nhut (*Jim Portis via Warren Thompson*)

and South Vietnam. As they were leaving the target area they heard, and then saw, a US Navy fighter get shot down. The A-1 pilots turned towards the site to see if they could assist, and the next thing Maj Thanh knew was that he had been hit by AAA. His engine immediately began to run rough, so he headed for the sea. Having managed to get some 20 miles off the coast, Maj Thanh was then forced to bail out. Once he landed in the water, he climbed into his raft. He remembered being more afraid of sharks than he was of the VC.

The following morning, a rescue helicopter came in to presumably pick up the US Navy pilot, but Maj Thanh said, 'They saw me first and came over to pick me up. They flew me out to the carrier, and then on to Da Nang'.

During his time with the 83rd SAG Maj Thanh was promoted to become the Skyraider group commander.

Fellow early A-1 pilot Capt Hoi Ba Tran flew with the 83rd alongside Maj Thanh in the mid-1960s. He recalled a particularly memorable operation that he undertook with the unit in March 1965. 'I was assigned to lead a group of three flights of four aircraft on an armed reconnaissance mission into southern North Vietnam'. The frag order stated that the A-1 pilots were to reconnoitre National Highway 1 (NH-1) from the DMZ to just south of Vinh. At this point they were to fly west to the Laotian border, then reverse course and intercept NH-1 again and proceed back to the DMZ. 'Along this route we were authorised to strike any military convoys, but strictly prohibited from striking any fixed installations. We were also forbidden to attack if we were fired on by these non-mobile installations', Capt Hoi explained.

He led his armed reconnaissance package north across the DMZ and ordered his flight into a tactical formation. The weather was clear, with unlimited visibility. Although Capt Hoi could see no military traffic on NH-1, they were fired upon. 'Tracers were suddenly coming up at us from what appeared to be a military unit not far from the side of the highway. The tracers were lagging behind us, so we proceeded north, performing minimum evasive manoeuvres as we went'. Hoi's flight headed north to the turnaround point, and after their excursion to the border and back, they proceeded south along NH-1 once again.

As the flight approached the location where they had previously been fired upon, Capt Hoi contacted 'Panama control' to ask permission to strike the site. Since they had still not seen any mobile military convoys to attack, the A-1 pilots felt that the AAA site that had engaged them seemed like a logical target. 'During the course of this mission there had been a chance that any one of us could have been shot down. We had also consumed a large quantity of fuel flying [for 300 miles] over enemy territory. Nevertheless, my request was denied', lamented Capt Hoi. Being the 'obedient soldier' that he was, he told his flight to join up once again and return to Da Nang. No ordnance had been expended during the entire mission.

A-1H 139690 sits on the ramp at Da Nang AB, which was frequently a staging base for missions into southern North Vietnam. Clearly visible is the fuselage emblem of the 83rd SAG, bearing the inscription *Than Phong*. This meant God of Wind or Kamikaze, as in Divine Wind – the typhoon that saved Japan from the invading Chinese in the 13th century. 'Than Phong' was also the radio call-sign used by the 83rd SAG (*John Dodson via Warren Thompson*)

With the influx of additional A-1s to the VNAF through MAP in 1965, the 522nd FS was created 'on paper' to accept additional Skyraiders that were actually destined for assignment to the 83rd SAG. Previously, the latter unit had used A-1s sourced from the 514th FS. From 1 April 1965 to 1 July 1967, 83rd SAG Skyraiders were administratively assigned to the 522nd FS, despite the latter having no operations building or personnel assigned to it. The unit did, however, 'possess' a squadron's worth of A-1H Skyraiders!

For political reasons, and perhaps because President Thieu feared the power that Col Ky held within the 83rd SAG, the unit was disbanded in January 1968.

It is difficult to determine just how many A-1s were lost by the 83rd SAG during the four years it operated Skyraiders from Tan Son Nhut AB because the unit's aircraft were initially borrowed from the 514th FS. Things became a lot clearer from 1 April 1965 with the establishment of the 522nd FS, as losses for the 83rd SAG from that date were set against the 'paper' unit. During this later period, the 83rd lost 13 A-1s and had six aircrew either killed or MIA. One of the men lost was USAF advisor Capt James C Wise Jr, whose aircraft was downed by enemy AAA on 23 December 1965 over Hua Nghia province, northwest of Saigon.

1st ACS

Appropriately, the first USAF Skyraider unit to be based in South Vietnam was the 1st ACS, which commenced operations with A-1Es at Bien Hoa AB from early June 1964. By year-end there were 48 Skyraiders at Bien Hoa AB, these machines belonging to a pool that both the 1st ACS and the co-located 602nd FS(C) drew from. Of significance is the fact that every one of these A-1Es wore VNAF markings due to the

Thirteen 'new' A-1Es awaiting delivery to Bien Hoa AB are parked on the ramp at NAS Cubi Point in the Philippines in 1964. Each Skyraider would fly local sorties from here prior to being ferried to Bien Hoa. 132619 survived its war with the USAF and was transferred to the VNAF in February 1971. No record of its loss exists (*Delmar Hilliard*)

sensitive political nature of US aircraft participating directly in the war against the VC.

Each Skyraider flew with a crew of two – either an American in the right seat with a Vietnamese student in the left, or an American flying the aeroplane in the left seat and a Vietnamese combat observer to his right. The requirement to fly with observers ended in March 1965,

Capt William May stands with his Vietnamese observer prior to departing on a mission from Qui Nhon in 1964. Two M64 GP bombs with 'Daisy Cutters' are loaded on the Inboard Stations while 12 M57s with 'Daisy Cutters' are loaded on the outboards. The 300-gallon tank would allow mission lengths approaching three hours. A power cable from the auxiliary power unit is plugged into the external power receptacle in the right wheel well to provide electrical power for engine start, although it was possible to start on battery power alone (*Larry Haight*)

Operations at Qui Nhon for the 34th TG were fraught with hazardous working conditions in close quarters. The large tent in the centre background was the operations centre that 'housed' the detachment leadership. The crew in the foreground is loading napalm onto the A-1E to left. One well-placed mortar round would have taken out the entire operation (*Tom Dwelle*)

although the latter were still used beyond that time. American Skyraiders also reverted to USAF markings at this time.

In February 1965 six A-1Es were permanently deployed to Qui Nhon – this number was soon increased to eight. Pilots typically spent two weeks deployed here (Qui Nhon was 220 nautical miles northeast of Bien Hoa), with aircraft being rotated back to Bien Hoa as maintenance requirements dictated. Col William Bethea, who was CO of the 34th Tactical Group (TG) during the early phase of USAF Skyraider operations in South Vietnam, wrote in a report to his higher headquarters;

'The runway and facilities are dangerous and the lighting facilities and navigation aids inadequate. The runway is 75 ft wide by 5000 ft long. The bomb and napalm dumps are right at the edge of the runway. I do not like any part of the whole operation. I consider it unsafe in every aspect.'

However, there was no doubt that having A-1Es at Qui Nhon increased the responsiveness of USAF air power in II Corps. If the strike had to come from Bien Hoa or Da Nang, the VC might have had time to melt away into the jungles and hills in many instances.

At the end of March 1965 Skyraiders from the 1st ACS participated in Operation *Sherwood Forest*, whose aim it was to clear the 'communist-infested' Boi Loi forest (long a sanctuary for enemy forces), some 25 miles west of Saigon. A US Forest Service representative was in Vietnam to oversee the operation, and to provide recommendations. For several weeks prior to the operation commencing, the area was saturated with 78,800 gallons of defoliation chemicals that would remove leaves from the foliage, thus making enemy troop movements more visible from the air – at least that was the theory.

Some 29 Skyraider sorties were flown, the aircraft dropping a total of 56 750-lb and 288 500-lb napalm tanks. In addition to this, B-57s dropped incendiary bombs and C-123s dropped drums of oil in the forest. The fires initially burned ferociously until the humid atmosphere was heated to the point that it produced a gigantic thundercloud. The subsequent rain deluge effectively put an end to the operation, leaving *Sherwood Forest* to be written off as a bad idea.

In June 1965 the 1st ACS became the first USAF squadron since the Korean conflict to receive a Presidential Unit Citation. It was awarded for the squadron's actions from 1 August 1964 to 15 April 1965, the 1st ACS having flown more than 1000 sorties and 17,000 flying hours during this

period. It had also expended an astonishing six million tons of ordnance. Deputy US Ambassador Alexis Johnson presented the award on 8 June 1965.

Losses were heavy in 1964-65, however, as the 1st ACS was operating its A-1Es within range of even the smallest AAA weapon, the AK-47 – and every VC had one of

Capt Don Emigholz flies formation on VNAF-marked USAF A-1E 132669 loaded with napalm and M47 WP bombs – South Vietnamese markings were worn by USAF A-1s until March 1965. This aircraft was lost during a RESCAP mission on 10 September that year, the A-1 crashing into the sea off Dong Hoi. Its pilot, Capt Graybill, bailed out and was subsequently rescued by a USAF HU-16 Albatross amphibious aircraft (*Don Emigholz*)

those, and a seemingly endless supply of ammunition. The A-1E was renowned for its ability to take a great deal of punishment, but it did have a few chinks in its armour. Beneath the engine cowling was the opening for the oil cooler. Rounds impacting in this location could result in loss of oil and eventual engine failure. Another weakness was the bottom of the wing beneath the ammunition cans that held the 20 mm rounds. If a round penetrated in this area, exploding ammunition could lead to a hydraulic fluid-fed fire that could eventually doom the aircraft.

The 3000 psi hydraulic lines to the aileron boost system and the wing-fold mechanism were in this area. Battle damage in either of these vulnerable locations could, and did, cause the loss of more than a few Skyraiders. In addition, pilots of these early A-1Es had no means of escape besides bailing out over the side, so crash-landings were a frequent occurrence.

This fate befell Capt Larry Haight and his Vietnamese observer on 17 April 1965, the pair flying with 1Lt R Y Costain on an air strike in the Can Tho area of Military Region I. Costain had rolled in for a napalm delivery and Haight was covering him with a strafing run when the latter felt rounds impacting his A-1E (133886) as the two pulled off the target. Costain, who could see oil streaming off Haight's Skyraider, recalled 'The whole underside and right side were thickly coated – it was even streaming off the tail'. Costain called 'Mayday' for the flight as Haight's big R-3350 was grinding to a halt. He was too low to bail out, so he looked for a level spot to land. He dropped the flaps and tried to slow as much as he could prior to hitting the ground. Costain was relieved to see Haight stagger out of the wreck of the A-1. 'Watching that thing hit and break up with the crew strapped inside was the most sickening thing I had ever observed. I thought that the aircraft was going to tip over', said Costain

Haight and his observer had made it out of the A-1 in one piece, but they were still in trouble as the enemy was closing in on their position. Haight had violated combat rule number one, as he later recalled. 'Don't land or bail out near the target you are bombing! Thankfully, "R Y" got an Army helicopter gunship in there to pick me up. He also kept those guys in "black pyjamas" from getting any closer than they did'.

A-1E 133886 is the object of interest for a throng of Vietnamese onlookers the day after Capt Larry Haight's crash-landing due to battle damage on 17 April 1965. A demolition team rigged the Skyraider with explosives and it was destroyed to deny its use to the enemy (*Larry Haight*)

Haight had suffered neck injuries and a broken right wrist during the crash-landing. 'When the engine broke off and rolled over the wing root, it tore off the front canopy and something caught my helmet and ripped it off. I also had compression fractures to five lower vertebrae and a broken right wrist from holding on to the stick when the bird hit the ground.'

Costain remembered the last time he had seen Haight on the ground;

'He was now out of the cockpit of the broken-in-half bird with his sidearm drawn, shooting in various directions where I assume he thought the VC was. His head was bent over, with his chin on his chest due to his broken neck. Haight had to be firing at sounds rather than by sight. Firing blindly, but fighting back!'

Capt Larry Haight was eventually rescued by an Army helicopter following his 140th, and final, A-1 Skyraider combat mission. He was evacuated on a medical flight out of the theatre, first to Clark AFB, in the Philippines, and later to Madigan Hospital in Tacoma, Washington, where he recuperated from his injuries.

MOVE TO PLEIKU

Following two false starts at the end of 1965, the 1st ACS moved to Pleiku AB in January 1966. The unit hit the ground running, and in the first six months of 1966, it flew 3538 combat missions lasting 9662 flying hours. But this torrid pace came with a heavy price. During this same period, the 1st ACS lost 13 aircraft and four men to enemy action. There were no 'milk runs' during this period of the war, the VC and NVA having stepped up their pressure in South Vietnam, and it seemed that everyone needed air support, day and night. Many times the Skyraiders were the only aircraft able to work under low overcasts. More and more FACs were asking for A-1s because of their accuracy and variety of weapons loads.

It was during this early period of 1st ACS operations from Pleiku that a USAF A-1 pilot flew arguably the most renowned of all Skyraider missions during the entire Vietnam War. The very short version of the story is that on 10 March 1966 Maj Bernie Fisher chose to land his A-1E (132649) under fire from enemy forces who held A-Shau airstrip in order to rescue Maj D W Myers, a fellow Skyraider pilot brought down (in 133867) by VC gunfire. Against all odds he accomplished just that.

I interviewed Col Bernard Fisher (retired) at a recent reunion of Skyraider pilots. I asked him what his thought process was as he formed the plan in

A-1G 132612 is de-armed after landing at Pleiku in 1967. Wearing the EC tail code of the 1st ACS at this time, the aircraft was transferred to the 6th ACS, also at Pleiku, in 1968, and was finally lost in northern Laos while flying with the 602nd FS(C) on 9 January 1970. Capt J L Hudson was making his fifth pass on enemy troops in mountainous territory 70 miles west of Sam Neua, in Houaphan province, when the A-1 was struck by small arms fire. He headed south but was forced to eject near Muang Poi. Hudson was quickly rescued by a USAF HH-53C from the 40th ARRS (*Tom Bigelow*)

Seven former 'Hobos' of the 1st SOS (ACS) pose with Medal of Honor recipient Bernie Fisher at the 1997 reunion of the A-1 Skyraider Association. They are, from left to right, Byron Hukee, Larry Gazzola, Roger Youngblood, Bernie Fisher, Bob Carlsen, Ron Smith and 'Buck' Buchanan (*Roger Youngblood via author's collection*)

his mind that he was going to land and pick up Maj Myers. He told me there were three things that led to his decision. The first was when he saw Myers run out of the ball of fire surrounding his aircraft and jump into a nearby ditch. The second was finding out that there would be no possibility of a rescue helicopter for at least the next 20 minutes. The third was that the other Skyraiders in the immediate area were providing solid support. All these things helped him to focus and build his plan. Once he made his decision, he landed, made the pickup and took off in well under ten minutes – probably more like seven or eight as far as he could remember. For this selfless act, Maj Bernie Fisher was awarded the Medal of Honor, thus becoming the first airman to earn America's highest military decoration during the Vietnam War.

MOVE TO NAKHON PHANOM

In December 1967 the 1st ACS left Pleiku for Nakhon Phanom RTAFB, becoming the first Skyraider unit to be permanently assigned to that airfield. A flight's worth of people (about 12 men, including pilots) remained behind at Pleiku to facilitate the arrival of the 6th ACS in February 1968. These personnel were subsequently assimilated by the 6th, remaining in South Vietnam as part of that unit.

The conditions at Nakhon Phanom were rather spartan in those early days, with a pierced-steel planking (PSP) runway and limited living accommodation. In time these were improved to become more than adequate. For example, in early 1969 the runway was paved with 8000 ft of concrete.

Photographed in 1968, this recently acquired A-1G 132528 is seen here loaded to the hilt at Pleiku. A genuine combat veteran, the aircraft was just commencing its second tour with the USAF after two previous tours with the VNAF. Its load here is nothing short of amazing – six CBU-14s, fours M47 WP bombs and two 500-lb and two 750-lb napalm tanks. Oh, and there is a 300-gallon Centreline Tank beneath the A-1's fuselage as well as 800 rounds of 20 mm ammunition in the wings. This was a ten-ton aeroplane on takeoff! Note the 'Flying Tiger' on the cowling, the AD-5W style rear canopy and the 'Playboy Bunny' on a single propeller blade – a trademark of early 34th TG Skyraiders. I flew this aircraft 15 times while it was with the 1st SOS at 'NKP 'in 1971-72. 132528 was transferred to the VNAF (for its third tour with the South Vietnamese) in November 1972, and it was one of 11 Skyraiders flown to Thailand on 30 April 1975. It belongs in a museum! (*Rob Cole*)

By October 1968 there were three A-1 squadrons operating at Nakhon Phanom, and with the 6th SOS at Pleiku, the high water mark (100+ aircraft) was reached for the USAF A-1 in Southeast Asia. This would soon change as the war seemingly began to wind down for the Air Force following the cessation of Operation *Rolling Thunder* on 1 November 1968. With the disbandment of the 602nd SOS on 31 December 1970, the 1st SOS

1Lt Art Baker flies over 'NKP' in A-1H 139608 at the end of yet another mission in July 1972. This aircraft was one of the final 19 'survivors' that were transferred to the VNAF in November 1972. There is no record of its fate (*Gary Koldyke*)

was the last remaining USAF Skyraider squadron in-theatre.

By October 1971 the 1st SOS could field 29 A-1s. In what was to be the unit's last year of operations, it would lose no fewer than ten aircraft.

Following three-and-half years of 'Vietnamization', where the onus on defending South Vietnam was progressively passed to the heavily re-equipped ARVN and VNAF, the renewed bombing offensive against North Vietnam, codenamed Operation *Linebacker*, from 10 May 1972 saw a dramatic spike in the number of US aircraft downed in enemy territory. The 1st SOS was called on to provide support for SAR missions generated to save downed aviators both north and south of the DMZ.

One of the more memorable rescue attempts from this period took place on 1-2 June 1972 following the shooting down of a Phantom II on the opening day of the *Linebacker I* offensive. F-4D 65-0784 of the 555th TFS/432nd TRW, call-sign 'Oyster 01', was the lead jet on a MiGCAP. During the pre-strike sweep portion of the mission, 'Oyster 01' shot down a MiG-21. Later, they themselves were shot down by an undetected MiG-19 60 miles west of Hanoi near Yen Bai airfield. Although the pilot, Maj Bob Lodge, did not escape the aircraft, the WSO, Capt Roger Locher, ejected and parachuted to safety, evading capture for 23 days.

Astonishingly, nothing was heard from either crewmember until 1 June. On that day, F-4s from the 555th TFS were again in the area, and they heard over the radio, 'Any US aircraft, this is "Oyster 01B", over'. A WSO in one of the Phantom IIs recognised the voice of Roger Locher and shouted over the intercom, 'My God, that is Roger Locher!' They answered his call and Locher replied, 'Hey guys, I've been down here a long time. Any chance of picking me up?' The reply of 'You bet there is' set the wheels in motion for the rescue of 'Oyster 01B'.

Capt Ron Smith from the 1st SOS was 'Sandy 01' that day, and his wingman and two Jolly Green HH-53s were orbiting on standby near the 'Fish's Mouth' on the border of Laos and North Vietnam when they got the call. They were only about 30 minutes south of the SAR location. Smith ordered the group north while they sought more information. Soon he arrived on the scene, with his Jolly Greens in tow, and 'parked' them in an orbit over the high ground southwest of Yen Bai airfield. What happened next got Smith's attention;

'As I started to turn back to the southeast, a MiG flew through the "Sandy 02" and Jolly holding pattern, then departed in my direction. "Sandy 02" did not fire at the MiG, stating later that he thought it was

another F-4, and that he did not have a clear shot because of the Jollys. I had everything that would "fire forward" armed on my aeroplane, but I never saw the MiG. I was close enough to Yen Bai to have put my gear down, turned final and landed. That is probably what the MiG was trying to do when he flew into the Jolly flight.'

After this close call, Smith determined that the survivor was hiding on the northeastern side of the valley. He duly crossed the Red River in order to reach 'Oyster 01B', and although he never actually saw Locher's position, Smith was confident that he knew where he was based on his now-stronger radio contact with the survivor. With light fading fast, he made the decision that a rescue could not be safely undertaken and headed south again, crossing the Red River and joining up with the rest of the SAR force as it headed back to base.

The next day, just before sunrise, Smith lead his SAR force north to Yen Bai. It would be a long flight to the SAR area – covering just three miles a minute gave all the aircrew involved plenty of time to collect their thoughts, as Yen Bai was more than 200 nautical miles from Nakhon Phanom. The plan, which had to be approved at the highest level of government, called for an attack against the communist airfield.

Capt Smith's wingman, Capt Buck Buchanan, more than proved his worth throughout this mission. Smith chose the same holding area as the previous day for the Jolly Greens, but took a different route to get there. Once in position, 'Sandy 01' and '02' set off across the Red River in search of 'Oyster 01B'. As they got within sight of Yen Bai airfield, they saw the impact and explosions of the bombs along its runway, which left it cratered in two places. Their task was to find the survivor. 'Oyster 01B' said he heard the 'Sandys' and Smith found him right away. He told Locher that they would be back in 30 minutes to pick him up, and that he was to flash his signal mirror at the first A-1 he saw when they returned. 'Sandy 01' and '02' then flew back across the Red River to bring the Jolly Greens in for the pickup.

'Sandy 01' and '02' led the SAR force across the Red River and proceeded into the area. Buchanan saw the mirror flash and told the survivor to 'pop' his 'smoke'. The Jolly Green soon saw the latter and slowed for the pickup. Once the survivor was on board, they headed south to cross the Red River Valley one last time. Once safely across, the force set course for Nakhon Phanom. Capts Ron Smith and Dale Stovall, who was the Jolly Green pickup pilot, were both awarded the Air Force Cross for their actions on 1-2 June 1972 during the 'Oyster 01B' SAR.

Five months later the 1st SOS handed over the last of its 19 A-1s to the VNAF, after which it became a squadron without aircraft. As a footnote to history, when *Linebacker II* operations commenced in December 1972, the 1st SOS signed out eight A-1s from the VNAF on hand-written receipts so that the unit could provide SAR coverage from Da Nang. Pilots were not allowed to conduct airborne alert orbits as they had done during *Linebacker I*,

The author snapped this photograph during his final Skyraider flight on 1 October 1972. These three aircraft, and the one flown by the author (A-1H 139791), were among the final 19 Skyraiders passed to the VNAF in November 1972. Pilots pictured are Capt 'Buck' Buchanan in A-1J 142058, 1Lt Tex Brown in A-1J 142028 and Capt Willy P Kramer in A-1H 135257 (*Byron Hukee*)

however, aircrew instead being forced to sit on the ground awaiting a SAR call. They were never scrambled.

The 1st ACS/SOS flew Skyraiders in combat from June 1964 to mid-November 1972 – longer than any other US A-1 squadron. During that period it lost 86 A-1s and had 42 aircrew either killed or listed as MIA. The first aircraft and pilot loss came on 29 August 1964 when Capt Richard D Goss was killed in the crash of A-1E 132465. The unit's last Skyraider loss came on 28 September 1972 when 1Lt Lance L Smith was shot down and rescued while flying A-1H 139738.

602nd FS(C)

The 602nd FS(C) was activated on 18 October 1964 under the control of the 34th TG at Bien Hoa AB. Its stated mission was to 'train the VNAF and augment its strike capability'. As previously mentioned in this chapter, the A-1Es assigned to the 34th carried both VNAF markings and observers in an attempt to mask overt US involvement in this ever-widening war. The observers, who were enlisted personnel from either the ARVN or VNAF, had little or no experience in aircraft, and most spoke little or no English. When being trained to fly the Skyraider, the VNAF upgrade pilot would be in either the right or left seat, depending on the phase of their training.

More than 50 per cent of the missions flown by the unit during this period were in the training category, as reported at the end of 1964. There were initially 20 qualified Skyraider pilots in the squadron, but by the end of the year this number had increased to 31. By March 1965, the requirement to carry a VNAF observer had been removed, and at the same time the markings worn by the Skyraiders of the 34th TG reverted to those of the USAF.

During the first six months of 1965, a total of 3235 sorties were flown in support of VNAF training. Of the 29 upgrade pilots assigned to the squadron for training, 13 were graduated as combat ready and assigned to operational VNAF A-1 squadrons.

Missions flown by the 602nd in direct support of the war effort were Air Alert, Air Cover, Interdiction, CAS, Helicopter Escort, Train Escort, Ship Escort and Aircraft Escort, the latter usually for C-123Ks performing *Ranch Hand* herbicidal spraying missions.

An early casualty for the 602nd FS(C), on 10 February 1965, was Capt William Duggan. He and his observer were in A-1E 132401 when it was hit during an attack on VC positions in the Mekong Delta area of South Vietnam. He had completed his bombing runs and was on his third strafing pass when the Skyraider was hit in the starboard wing by heavy-calibre AAA. The aircraft shuddered and Duggan attempted to make it to the coast, where he would have a better chance of being rescued.

With its wing on fire, the damaged A-1 was unable to maintain altitude, forcing Duggan to order the observer to bail out. Once the latter had

This Bien Hoa-based A-1E is heading out on a training mission with a Vietnamese student in the left seat and an American instructor in the right. The VNAF markings belie the fact that this is a Skyraider assigned to the 34th TG. The 48 A-1Es assigned to the group were in a common pool, which meant that they were flown by pilots of either the 1st ACS or the 602nd FS(C) (*Richard Keogh*)

jumped, Duggan looked for a place to crash-land, as he was now too low to bail out. He ditched about 100 yards off the beach and was able to egress safely and make it ashore. Duggan crossed the beach and entered a grassy area for concealment. He buried himself in the sand and vegetation and listened while a VC search party moved into his area. A rescue helicopter soon arrived, however, scattering the communist troops. Duggan established contact with the helicopter and quickly climbed aboard when it landed nearby. The observer's parachute was located, but the man could not be found. Duggan subsequently perished on 31 December 1971 when his Phantom II crashed during a night mission over Laos.

Pictured in front of the Da Nang Officers' Club are the seven pilots from the 34th TG that participated in the raid against North Vietnam on 8 February 1965. They are, from left to right, Capts Al Bache, Jay Longnecker and Shelley Hilliard, Lt Col Andy Chapman and Capts Charley Gulley, Al Motley Jr and Dean Werely (*Delmar Hilliard*)

FLAMING DART

Two days prior to Capt Duggan being downed over the Mekong Delta, Lt Col Andrew Chapman, the first CO of the 602nd, led an element of six A-1E Skyraiders from the 34th TG as part of Operation *Flaming Dart* – a series of reprisal air strikes against target areas in North Vietnam. These missions were flown by both USAF and VNAF aeroplanes in response to a deadly VC mortar attack on Camp Holloway, near Pleiku, in the central highlands of South Vietnam, in the early hours of 7 February. Lt Col Chapman gave the following description of the mission a short time after it was completed;

'We staged out of Da Nang and were part of a joint 30-aeroplane VNAF/USAF Skyraider package. The VNAF Skyraiders launched first, followed by our six A-1Es. For this mission we had the Vietnamese insignia removed from the aircraft and replaced with US markings. After takeoff, we proceeded at low-level up the coast to avoid early warning detection. Once past Hue, we cut inland, going in just over the flat tableland of the foothills. We remained at or below 100 ft above the ground this entire time.

'Once in the target area, we could see the smoke generated by the flak suppression strikes of the F-100s. Our entire six-aeroplane package was on and off the target in less than a minute. Each of our Skyraiders carried eight 500-lb and four 250-lb bombs, which were all released in one pass. Following our deliveries, we egressed to the east at maximum power and low altitude to a point about four miles off the coast, where we turned south to parallel the coast for our return to Da Nang.'

Skyraider tactics were a 'work in progress' at this early point in the war. For day missions, the standard tactic was to fly four-ship formations. The first element would carry bombs and the second element would carry napalm. All aircraft were loaded with 20 mm ammunition. Aircraft Nos 1 and 2 would strike first with their bombs, normally making two passes each, while 3 and 4 held high waiting their turn. The elements would then change positions, allowing 3 and 4 to make two passes for their napalm deliveries. Following this, all aircraft would make one or two strafing passes.

On 16 May 1965 one of the worst flightline disasters of the entire war occurred at Bien Hoa AB when Mk 82 bombs loaded onto B-57 bombers inexplicably exploded, resulting in the destruction of a multitude of aircraft and the loss of 27 American lives. Estimates vary as to the exact number of aircraft destroyed, but at least 11 VNAF A-1 Skyraiders were considered to be combat losses (*Delmar Hilliard*)

Night missions, which were flown in two-ship formations, typically involved strip alert so as to provide on-call defence for isolated forts manned by US Special Forces. Many of the forts were located in remote areas away from the main bodies of US forces. The enemy knew this, and would usually bide their time until the weather was bad before launching an attack at night. 1Lt Tom Dwelle, who flew 370 combat missions (totalling more than 600 hours) in the Skyraider, said he could never remember a time that they cancelled a mission due to weather.

ARVN forts and Special Forces compounds used a device known as a 'fire arrow' to indicate the direction from which they were being attacked. A large arrowhead made of wood was mounted on a swivel parallel to the ground, with fuel-filled tin cans placed along the shaft and barbs of the arrow. During a night attack on the fort, the fuel was set alight and the arrow pointed in the direction of enemy troops. The 'fire arrow' was so effective as a reference point for air support that it was possible to make an attack in an A-1 without the aid of a dedicated flare ship.

Missions for the 602nd during the early months of 1965 were normally conducted in the neighbouring III and IV Corps military regions, while the detachment at Qui Nhon covered I and II Corps. But the initiation of Operation *Rolling Thunder* on 2 March 1965 and the subsequent bombing of targets in North Vietnam meant that aircraft losses would steadily increase as more and more SAR missions were flown.

A first-of-its-kind mission for this period was flown on 27 July 1965, when the 602nd's Capt John Larrison led a four-ship flight from Bien Hoa to Udorn RTAFB for what turned out to be the first out-of-country deployment for the unit's A-1Es. Upon landing at the Thai base, the pilots were immediately taken to the SAR operations HQ, where they were given a detailed briefing on the disastrous air strikes that had been flown earlier that day against SA-2 'Guideline' surface-to-air missile (SAM) sites around Hanoi – the first such attacks of the conflict, which had seen six F-105Ds shot down.

The A-1 pilots were told that their mission was to provide low altitude air cover just west of Hanoi for SAR operations. There was an airborne command post directing activities and jet aircraft providing high cover and MiGCAP. They were to stay low, as the SAMs then in use were ineffective below 5000 ft. However, at that lower altitude small arms and AAA fire became more effective.

Early the next morning two A-1s were placed on strip alert, with the remaining two aircraft serving as backups. That afternoon, while Capt Larrison and his wingman were on strip alert, word came through that a US Navy pilot (Lt(jg) G R Townsend) had been forced to eject from his A-4 Skyhawk following premature detonation of his bombs over a target in southern North Vietnam. A good 'chute had been seen by his wingmen and contact had been made with the pilot on the ground.

A rescue mission was underway and helicopters were en route to the site. The A-1s were scrambled to provide low air cover for the pickup. The Skyraider pilots encountered a low deck of broken clouds, which they hoped would hide them from the AAA. It was less than an hour to the SAR site.

As the A-1s approached the area they found out that two USAF H-43s flying from a forward base in Laos had already arrived on site, and the lead helicopter was coming out with the downed pilot aboard. Larrison and his wingman took up escort positions as the H-43s headed west for home. On the way back, by monitoring radio calls between the helicopters and the airborne SAR command and control aircraft, the A-1 pilots determined that the H-43s were flying to their home base of Nakhon Phanom (irreverently dubbed 'Naked Fanny' by US servicemen). The two Skyraiders landed there also due to their low fuel states.

Lt(jg) Townsend was quickly taken to the fight surgeon on base for a check over, and after getting two small bandages applied to cuts on his forehead, he was discharged. Anxious to return to his squadron (VA-23, embarked aboard USS *Midway* [CVA-41]), Townsend accepted the offer of a lift as far as Udorn from Larrison – the Naval Aviator duly rode in the right seat of one of the A-1Es. After a further two days of airborne alert, but without any additional SAR commitments, the four Skyraiders were flown back to Bien Hoa.

A few weeks after the flight had returned home, the 602nd FS(C) set up a two-week SAR rotation of four aircraft into Udorn. The initial purpose of this detachment was to provide low altitude air cover for SAR operations in North Vietnam and Laos. What Capt Larrison did not know at the time was that the temporary duty commitment to Udorn would rapidly expand in size, and the entire 602nd FS(C) would move there a little over a year later.

It was also during this period that the radio call-sign 'Sandy' became synonymous with the A-1 Skyraider SAR mission. Although several groups of pilots had flown SAR missions out of Udorn by late 1965, they had not utilised the 'Sandy' call-sign. Its first appearance came near year-end when Capt W J 'Doc' George led four replacement A-1Es to Udorn. His Bien Hoa departure call-sign had been 'Sandy', and upon the flight's arrival at Udorn, 'Doc' was asked what call-sign he would like to use while there. His reply, 'Sandy', subsequently spread theatre-wide to become the A-1's SAR call-sign until war's end.

During the second half of 1965 the 602nd flew many of its sorties from Udorn. On 6 November 1965, while flying from the base, two 'Sandys' were downed during a SAR mission over North Vietnam. Capt Richard Bolstad (in 132469) and Capt George McKnight (in 132439) were both hit by large-calibre AAA while searching for a downed F-105D pilot who had been lost near Phu Ban the previous day. Altogether, this ultimately fruitless SAR effort (the Thunderchief pilot, Lt Col G C McCleary, had been killed when his jet was hit by a SAM) led to the loss of two helicopters and two Skyraiders, plus damage to four

Part of the Skyraider lineup for the 602nd FS(C) at Nha Trang in March 1966. This photograph shows a mix of newly camouflaged A-1s parked alongside those in their original markings. The letters on the engine cowl were an aid for maintenance personnel so that they could tell at a distance which Skyraider was parked where. The A-1 in the foreground boasts a skull and crossbones symbol on its fin in an early attempt at individualisation of aircraft by the 602nd. The two nearest Skyraiders are loaded with two M47 WP and 12 M30 GP bombs (*Don Wilkerson*)

other A-1s, together with the loss of five airmen. All five downed on 6 November became POWs, but were returned in 1973 during Operation *Homecoming*.

During its first 14 months of operations up to 31 December 1965, the 602nd FS(C) lost 15 Skyraiders and had eight pilots who were either killed or MIA. But A-1s were not the only aircraft suffering high levels of attrition. In 1964-65, 434 VNAF and USAF fixed wing (non-helicopter) aircraft were lost in Southeast Asia, with 400 aircrew either killed or MIA. Not all who were shot down perished, however, for in 1965 alone there were 127 aircrew rescued by SAR forces.

MOVE TO NHA TRANG

With ramp space becoming limited at Bien Hoa AB by early 1966, the 602nd relocated to Nha Trang AB on 1 February that year. The method of movement employed by the unit was nothing short of remarkable. Pilots simply loaded their personal belongings into the 'blue rooms' of their A-1Es that had already been loaded with ordnance. They then took off on their combat missions, struck their targets (despite personal reel-to-reel tape decks and A-3 kit bags rattling around in the 'blue room' as the Skyraiders were manoeuvred aggressively in the target area!) and recovered at Nha Trang. Everything but the squadron's oversized items was moved by A-1Es in this fashion.

What is truly remarkable is that in the first three months of 1966, the squadron flew 2839 combat sorties and 6062 combat hours from four different locations (Nha Trang AB, Qui Nhon AB, Udorn RTAFB and Nakhon Phanom RTAFB). Capt Bill Prescott joined the 602nd at this time;

'When I arrived in the squadron, it was operating from four bases. The four flights in the squadron (A, B, C and D) rotated between each location on a regular basis. The rotation went something like two weeks at Qui Nhon, two weeks at Nha Trang, two weeks at Udorn, six weeks at Nha Trang and then it started all over again. At the time the primary mission at Udorn was SAR alert, with four aircraft here and four at "NKP", along with two Jolly Greens at each location. The operation at "NKP" was actually a detachment from the detachment at Udorn.'

The latter base officially became home for the 602nd in December 1966, although its A-1s and their support personnel had actually moved from Nha Trang eight months earlier. According to Capt Prescott, 'in late April the entire 602nd FS(C) moved to Udorn on a "permanent TDY" basis, and the Nha Trang and Qui Nhon operations for the 602nd ceased. We had "variations authorised" marked on our TDY orders, so we could legally rotate to "NKP" for SAR alert. We were still permanently assigned to the 14th Air Commando Wing at Nha Trang, however'.

The pilots of 'C' Flight of the 602nd FS(C) pose for a photograph before departing Nha Trang at the start of a deployment to Udorn in early 1966. They are, from left to right, Capts Ben Skelton, Bill Prescott, Win DePoorter and Jim Ingalls, 1Lt Butch Viccellio, Maj Ken McArn and Capt Zack Pryse. Ingalls was rescued after being shot down over northeastern Laos in A-1E 133871 on 1 May 1966 (*Bill Prescott*)

What this meant was that after less than three months at Nha Trang, following its move from Bien Hoa, the 602nd had moved yet again as a direct result of the increasing tempo of *Rolling Thunder*, and the growing losses associated with the offensive.

These were the 'wild west' days of SAR in Southeast Asia, and there was a very steep learning curve for the units involved. Indeed, seemingly every possible search and rescue technique was tried at least once during this early war period, which ultimately meant that everything we did in the 'Sandy' role from 'NKP' in 1971-72 had been developed by the 'original' A-1 crews at Udorn in the 1966-70 timeframe. Just when we thought we were the first to use this tactic or that technique, we would find out that the guys at Udorn had pioneered it back in 1966-67.

Having flown the A-1H on 'Sandy' SAR missions well into North Vietnam, I cannot imagine going way up north in the 'Fat Face' A-1E, with its reduced visibility, and doing it again and again, day after day until you got to 100 missions north of the DMZ, at which point you got to go home. But many pilots never went home. The loss rate during the early years of the 'Sandy' mission was the heaviest in the Skyraider community for the entire war.

One of the more interesting but lesser known missions performed by the 602nd from Udorn in 1966-67 was armed FAC. Presumably the theory was that the A-1 could conduct this vital task in areas where the threat level was deemed to be too high for a typical FAC aircraft to survive. By carrying out this hazardous mission, the A-1 pilots may well have been the precursors to the F-100 *Misty* Fast FACs of later years. The F-4 subsequently assumed the Fast FAC role. Bill Prescott explained;

'While I was at Udorn the A-1s flew using three call-signs – "Sandy", "Firefly" and "Dragonfly". "Sandy" was (and still is throughout the USAF) the SAR call-sign, while "Firefly" and "Dragonfly" were used for armed reconnaissance, interdiction and armed FAC roles. The area the mission was fragged to usually determined which of the latter two call-signs was used. Missions going north out of Udorn to northern Laos and some areas of North Vietnam used "Firefly", while missions to the east into the southern Laotian panhandle and Route Pack I of southern North Vietnam used "Dragonfly".'

MOVE TO 'NKP'

The 602nd, though no stranger to 'NKP', was officially moved there on a permanent basis on 1 July 1968. Exactly a month later the squadron designation changed from Fighter Squadron (Commando) to Special Operations Squadron. This was seen as a 'double whammy' by more than a few of the pilots in the 602nd, one of whom explained that 'we were upset about the move and redesignation. We saw it as a political thing, and we always considered ourselves to be air commandos in a fighter squadron, despite our new name. And we knew that things would be worse at "NKP", where we would be co-located with the 56th Special Operations Wing (SOW)'.

I can attest to the fact that operating at a separate location from your wing leadership definitely has its advantages, as you are not under the daily close scrutiny of the wing. This in turn means that you can operate much more freely.

Yet another reason for discontent amongst pilots at this time was the fact that the 602nd had to start sharing 'Sandy' missions with the other two A-1 squadrons at 'NKP'. Up until then, all 'Sandy' sorties had been flown by the 602nd out of Udorn and 'NKP'.

The 602nd's CO throughout this period was Lt Col William A Jones III, who on 1 September 1968 became the second A-1 pilot to be awarded the Medal of Honor for his bravery under fire. Flying A-1H 139738 as the on-scene commander in the dawn rescue of F-4D pilot Capt J R Wilson near Dong Hoi, in North Vietnam, Lt Col Jones remained on station until he sighted the survivor, despite his Skyraider being repeatedly hit by heavy and accurate AAA.

Upon reaching the area in which the badly injured Capt Wilson was sheltering, he made several low passes across a valley and spotted the downed pilot near a towering rock formation. Enemy gunners occupying a position near the top of the formation opened fire on Lt Col Jones, who quickly realised that the AAA battery had to be destroyed before a rescue could be made. He attacked the position with cannon and rocket fire.

While making his second pass, his aircraft was hit and the cockpit set ablaze. He attempted to eject but the damaged extraction system failed (its rocket motor had been ignited by shrapnel), only jettisoning the canopy. Before the fire died out, Lt Col Jones was badly burned. Despite searing pains from severe burns sustained on his arms, hands, neck, shoulders and face, Lt Col Jones pulled his A-1 into a climb and attempted to transmit the location of the downed pilot and the enemy gun position to the other aircraft in the area. His calls were blocked by other pilots' transmissions, repeatedly directing him to bail out, and within seconds his transmitters were disabled and he could receive only on one channel.

Lt Col Jones returned to base, and, despite his severe burns, landed his damaged aircraft safely and insisted on passing on the vital information concerning the downed pilot's exact location before receiving medical treatment. Capt Wilson was rescued later that day.

Sadly, William Jones perished in the crash of a private aircraft in the USA on 15 November 1969 before he could be presented with his Medal of Honor.

The 602nd also played a pivotal role in what would ultimately turn out to be one of the largest SAR efforts of the entire war in terms of A-1 sorties flown. Downed during the late forenoon of 5 December 1969, 'Boxer 22A' (Capt B F Danielson) and 'Boxer 22B' (1Lt W J Bergeron) had ejected from

A-1H 139779 sports the TT tail code of the 602nd SOS while patrolling on a 'Sandy' mission in December 1969. The aircraft is armed with dual SUU-11 mini-guns, four 20 mm cannons and four LAU-3 rocket pods, thus giving the pilot plenty of forward-firing ordnance to employ should he need to. The mission load-out also includes two 500-lb napalm tanks. The red-tipped white cones on the LAU-3 dispensers were made of lightweight cardboard, and they broke away when the first rocket left the pod. Apparently there was a shortage of nose cones at 'NKP' at this time as the rockets in the pod on station 12 are exposed to the elements. No doubt the pilot set a 'couple of clicks' of left rudder trim to offset the drag created by the pod (*Don Engebretsen*)

their F-4C after the jet was hit by a 37 mm AAA shell whilst pulling up from its bombing run over the Mu Gia Pass in Laos. The crew came down only a few miles from their target – never a good thing. In fact the only good thing about this location was its close proximity to 'NKP', where all the SAR forces were based. It was but a 20-minute flight for the 'Sandys' in their A-1s, the Jolly Greens in their HH-53s and the 'Nail' FACs in their OV-10s.

Heavy ground fire was encountered as the SAR forces entered the area, and an early attempt at a pickup saw the Jolly Greens having to retreat without the survivors after suffering serious battle damage. Five more attempts were similarly repelled by heavy AAA, with the final effort being made at last light. The survivors, who had landed less than 200 yards apart on either side of a river in a valley, were 'put to bed' after being briefed to be ready in the morning for a first-light rescue attempt.

With dawn approaching on 6 December, the SAR forces launched to the SAR area. The 'Nail' FAC had departed earlier to establish contact with the survivors, and to determine the situation on the ground. 'Boxer 22A' had revealed his position when he popped his signal smoke during the final pickup attempt the day before, and he now reported enemy troops in his vicinity searching for him. About mid-morning 'Boxer 22B' reported gunfire coming from across the river in the vicinity of 'Boxer 22A'. Capt Danielson was never heard from again. Full attention was now directed toward the recovery of 'Boxer 22B', but despite their best efforts, each pickup attempt was met with heavy gunfire directed at the Jolly Greens.

A number of the large-calibre weapons defending the area were housed in caves in a nearby karst, so F-4s were called in to target the guns with Paveway I laser-guided bombs. At one point during the day 'Boxer 22B' reported enemy troops within ten metres of his position – these were quickly despatched by the 'Sandys' in a precision strafing run. Despite the best efforts of the F-4s and A-1s, intensive ground fire continued to keep the Jolly Greens at bay every time they were brought in for a pickup attempt. After trying a total of five times, the SAR team once again had to tell 1Lt Bergeron to 'hole up' for the night.

As dawn approached on 7 December, the SAR forces headed to the Mu Gia Pass once again. With this area being deemed to be far too dangerous to attack during the day, most pilots working the SAR had never seen it during daylight hours. What they saw was 'like the surface of the moon' said one, the Mu Gia Pass having been identified as a key choke point on the Ho Chi Minh Trail.

When the 'Nail' FAC once again established initial contact with 'Boxer 22B', he said he had moved, and that he could hear searchers near his old location. The first order of business was to strike that position. As the morning progressed, it at last seemed that there was less ground fire than the day before. Now, as AAA came up, it was dealt with in short order. By mid-morning, preparations had been made for yet another pickup attempt. Skyraiders carrying CBU-22s were used to screen the survivor's area and protect the Jolly Green while it was in the hover. CS gas-filled CBU-19s were also employed to discourage movement on the ground. Finally, the stage was set and the execute command was given. Following what seemed like an eternity yet was but a few minutes, the Jolly Green started to climb away from the hover, the pilot radioing that 'the survivor is on board. Now let's get the hell out of here'.

1Lt 'Jink' Bender poses with 1Lt Woody Bergeron ('Boxer 22B') shortly after the latter had returned to 'NKP' following his dramatic – and lengthy – rescue from Ban Phanop, near the Mu Gia Pass, on 7 December 1969. Phantom II WSO Bergeron had ejected near Route 23 of the Ho Chi Minh Trail – one of the most heavily defended areas along the entire trail network. There were 171 A-1 and 24 HH-53 Jolly Green sorties flown during the three-day SAR effort for Bergeron (*'Jink' Bender*)

The SAR for 'Boxer 22B' was arguably the most concentrated application of air power in one area for the longest time during the entire Vietnam War – 51 hours for the rescue of 1Lt 'Woody' Bergeron from Mu Gia Pass. During this period some 171 'Sandy' sorties, 24 Jolly Green sorties, 25 'Nail' sorties and innumerable other support missions had been flown as part of the rescue effort. Sadly, one PJ had been killed during the third failed pickup attempt on 5 December, and 'Boxer 22A', Capt B F Danielson, was MIA (later changed to KIA). Twelve A-1s and at least eight HH-53s had suffered battle damage during this SAR.

The 602nd had pioneered the 'Sandy' SAR mission and operated in high-threat areas day after day. Its performance in the 18 months between mid-1965 through to the end of 1966 was awe-inspiring. Although no official statistics are available, the unit was surely responsible for saving the lives of scores of aircrew and other personnel needing rescue. This performance came at a devastating price, however. From 1 June 1965 to 31 December 1966 the 602nd lost 35 A-1s and had 20 pilots either killed or MIA, with three more listed as POWs. By the time the squadron was inactivated on 31 December 1970 its total losses had risen to 77 aircraft and 38 pilots killed or MIA.

USAF A-1 TRAINING SQUADRONS

The units that trained most USAF and VNAF A-1 pilots are something of an enigma. This is because the squadron tasked with carrying out the programme had no fewer than five different designations during the nine-year existence of the 'Skyraider school' at Hurlburt Field. Some of these changes involved simply renaming the existing squadron, but others saw entirely different units assuming the training duties.

Part of the reason for this was due to the relocation of the A-1 training squadron's two parent units from January 1966 to July 1969. The 1st Air Commando Wing (ACW) was initially located at Hurlburt Field, but it then moved to England AFB in Louisiana, only to return to Hurlburt Field, where it still exists today as the 1st SOW. The 4410th Combat Crew Training Wing, conversely, was formed at England AFB, before relocating to Hurlburt Field and then returning to England AFB. Despite these movements, the one constant through the entire nine years was that Skyraider training was always done at Hurlburt Field.

The first two USAF units to conduct A-1 training were the 603rd and 604th FS(C)s, both forming on 1 July 1963. These squadrons were assigned to the newly designated 1st ACW, also located at Hurlburt Field.

Training started slowly as the 'system' was still gearing up to modify ex-US Navy Skyraiders into what would become known as the 'USAF A-1E standard'. In addition to the two A-1Es 'borrowed' from the US Navy for the Skyraider evaluation, five additional unmodified E-models were acquired to form an early nucleus of seven A-1Es available to train USAF pilots.

Delivered to the 1st ACW at the very end of 1964, A-1E 135036 is prepared for static display at Langley AFB, Virginia, in May 1965. Still looking 'showroom fresh', the Skyraider has been loaded with six LAU-3 rocket pods, two 750-lb napalm tanks and a 300-gallon Centerline fuel tank. Note the stack of nose cones for the rocket pods in front of the aircraft (*Merle Olmsted via author's collection*)

Once USAF-modified Skyraiders began to arrive in mid-June 1964, the unmodified A-1Es were sent to McClellan AFB for modification (see also page 11).

After a very brief existence, the 604th FS(C) was disbanded on 8 November 1964, leaving the 603rd as the sole A-1 training squadron. In another change, the latter squadron was re-designated the 603rd ACS.

The early non-modified Skyraiders boasted only a single set of flight controls for the occupant of the left seat. To say that there was concern about putting instructor pilots in the right seat with no possibility of assisting the student with control of the aircraft would be a gross understatement. The wing history from 1964 stated, 'The IPs are really along for the ride since they can do nothing but advise. It is only a matter of time, with such improper equipment, until a trainee will lose control'. But the commitment to rapidly produce qualified Skyraider pilots overrode the safety concerns of those conducting the training.

The 'Skyraider school' was originally scheduled to receive the 31st and 32nd A-1Es to be modified, with the Pacific Air Force getting the first 30. This was later changed to the 16th and 17th modified airframes, and they went into service at Hurlburt Field in June 1964. The 603rd ACS possessed 18 Skyraiders by year-end, only two of which had been modified with dual controls. By December 1965 the unit's fleet of Skyraiders had grown in number to 34 A-1Es – presumably the 16 additional aircraft were all modified dual-control Skyraiders.

Under the heading of 'be careful what you ask for', the USAF had to temporarily suspend deliveries of additional Skyraiders to Hurlburt Field because of inadequate ramp space to park them. The 603rd ACS history for late 1965 stated, however, that the upcoming move of the 1st ACW to England AFB in January 1966 was expected to alleviate the problem, so deliveries could resume.

An additional snag that impacted training during this early period was the availability of bombing ranges for weapons delivery training. The A-1s were given the lowest priority for the use of such facilities, resulting in students having to delay their graduations from 'Skyraider school' until they had completed the specified number of weapons delivery sorties. I know from experience that this problem never went away, as courses were being delayed for exactly the same reason as late as 1971 when I received my Skyraider training.

Despite safety concerns, approximately 38 USAF pilots completed the A-1 conversion course in 1964 during the first full year of training at Hurlburt Field. This number would grow to more than 100 as the training fleet of Skyraiders grew during 1965. From early 1966 the VNAF began to send selected pilots to Hurlburt Field for Skyraider training too. Typically, they first attended a T-28 course at Randolph AFB, Texas, where they earned their VNAF pilot's wings, before coming to Hurlburt Field. Their course

A-1E 133906 hangs on the wing of a second Skyraider as the aircraft fly over the Eglin range complex in December 1965. The relatively clean appearance of the A-1 would indicate that this was one of the first Skyraiders to appear in this paint scheme – it was delivered to Hurlburt on 10 October 1965. Carrying just a single, empty, LAU-59 rocket pod, this aircraft is almost certainly returning from a gunnery training mission (*Herb Meyr*)

A-1E 132655 rests between flights on the ramp at Hurlburt Field in September 1967. The AD tail code identifies it as a Skyraider assigned to the 1st ACW. Note the gust lock at the base of the rudder, which protected it from being damaged due to winds while parked (*Ron Picciani via author's collection*)

lasted about four months, during which time they would log approximately 40 hours of Skyraider flight time. A typical course for American pilots was about one month shorter, with 30 hours of flight time.

In addition to its primary training mission, the A-1 unit was frequently called upon to provide aircraft for 'firepower demonstrations', most often at night. Herb Meyr, who was an IP at Hurlburt from 1966 to 1969, recalled an incident that happened to him while leading one of these firepower 'demos'. The time-on-target (TOT) was scheduled late enough that it was nighttime when he took off. Just after departure he experienced a complete electrical failure, after which it was not only dark outside the aircraft, but the same inside too! Meyr quickly grabbed his flashlight in order to see the instruments so that he could maintain control. He could not tell anyone of his problem since his radios were inoperative, and no one could see him since all his external lights were off. Meyr found out later that many of his colleagues thought he had crashed after takeoff.

Climbing away from Hurlburt Field, he circled the base as the rest of the formation took off – there were several other types of aircraft participating in the 'demo', so he watched as they all took off. Once everyone had departed, Meyr cautiously descended and lined up with the runway to make a low pass so that the tower would see him. He could see all the flashing red lights on the field from the fire trucks that had been alerted to a possible downed aircraft. Meyr made his low pass and pushed up the throttle so that if they did not see him, they would at least hear him.

Standard procedure for such an emergency was to make the low pass and then come around and land, while watching for a green light from the tower. Meyr saw no green light, but he could see that the runway was clear, so he landed. No one had seen him land, including the fire trucks on the taxiways near the runway. He taxied carefully off the runway and pulled directly in front of a fire truck. Only then did anyone realise that the aircraft they thought had crashed had actually just landed. Meyr motioned for the fire truck to lead him in to the parking area, where the lighting on the ramp finally made him visible. Having parked the aircraft, he jumped into the spare A-1 that was loaded and ready to go. A short time later Meyr rejoined his flight and made both the TOT and the firepower 'demo'.

A-1E 135042 sports an AH code and a TAC crest on its fin, as well as the emblem of the 1st SOW on the engine cowl. The AH code was used from late 1971 through to the end of the 'Skyraider school' in November 1972. One of the oldest A-1s at Hurlburt, 135042 survived eight years of service as a training aircraft until it was eventually transferred to the VNAF in late 1972. I flew this A-1 twice during my training course at Hurlburt in 1971 (*Author's collection*)

Skyraider pilot training at Hurlburt Field peaked in 1969 when approximately 200 USAF and VNAF pilots completed their courses. The final history report for the 4407th CCTS showed that the unit trained a total of 625 pilots. In total, more than 1000 pilots graduated from the 'Skyraider school' at Hurlburt Field in the nine years of the training programme's existence. The final A-1 left the base bound for McClellan AFB on 28 October 1972, the aircraft being flown by the squadron commander of the 4407th CCTS, Lt Col Davis Glass.

The training units at Hurlburt Field flew the A-1 from mid-1963 through to late October 1972, and during that time there were 15 Skyraiders lost resulting in the deaths of 13 pilots. This high ratio of aeroplanes lost to pilots killed is due to the fact that the majority of the sorties flown saw the A-1s dual manned, with two pilots in the aircraft.

This photograph was taken in April 1971 when a plaque honouring the Medal of Honor mission of Bernie Fisher was dedicated at Hurlburt Air Park – it remains on display there today. Pictured from left to right are Col Bernard Fisher, Lt Col Davis Glass (4407th CCTS commander) and Col Michael Horgan (1st SOW commander). Fisher flew his now legendary mission over the A Shau Valley on 10 March 1966 (*USAF via Davis Glass*)

FOLLOW-ON SKYRAIDER UNITS

S kyraider units were particularly active during the middle years of the Vietnam War, with USAF squadrons heavily tasked flying SAR missions in support of Operation *Rolling Thunder* and their VNAF counterparts helping the ARVN in its fight against the VC south of the DMZ.

One of the latter units was the 516th FS, which had initially been formed as the 2nd FS at Nha Trang AB in December 1961. Exactly two years later the squadron became the 516th FS. Initially equipped with T-28 Trojans, it received Skyraiders following a move to Da Nang AB in 1964. This re-location was prompted by the pressing need for A-1 support in northern South Vietnam, as Military Region I was always busy due to its location alongside the DMZ.

During this period, the training of VNAF Skyraider pilots was still being undertaken by USAF instructors of the 34th TG at Bien Hoa. Future 516th FS pilot 1Lt Nguyen Quoc Dat recalled his welcome home when he reported for duty following his T-28 training in the USA in 1964;

'After we returned to Vietnam we reported to Gen Nguyen Ngoc Loan, the deputy commander-in-chief of the VNAF. He greeted us with a big smile, before telling our group "I know you all want to be fighter pilots. Congratulations, your wish has been granted!" The VNAF desperately needed fighter pilots at this time, so we knew that there were no other choices available to us!

'We reported to the 1st ACS, followed by US Navy squadron VA-152, for training. Phase I was conducted by the USAF. We had no specific

Two A-1Hs from the 516th FS fly in close formation on the lead Skyraider as they approach Da Nang AB for landing. Lt Nguyen Dat, wearing his 'Rising Sun' flight helmet, is flying the nearest Skyraider. Note the *GROSS_____* marking at the bottom of the engine cowl – a leftover from the aircraft's time with the US Navy conducting carrier operations, where the gross weight of the aircraft was used for catapult settings. A-1H 139796 in the background was a combat loss on 25 November 1968 while in service with the 514th FS (*Unknown photographer via Nguyen Dat*)

A-1H 135325 sits on a PSP pad at Chu Lai AB in early 1965. At this time Chu Lai had but a 1200-metre long PSP runway. The VNAF pilot who landed this aircraft following an in-flight emergency was no doubt happy to find this much runway. 135325 was lost in a fatal landing accident at Da Nang on 12 June 1965 (*Don Yates via Martin Halpin collection*)

instructor assigned to train us, but we would take part in combat missions in the A-1E, with a different USAF pilot each time. He would do all the flying from the left seat and we would watch him from the right seat, trying to learn as much as we could. The US Navy conducted gunnery training in Phase II. Initially, we familiarised ourselves with the A-1H, and after a few "touch-and-go" landings, a Naval Aviator would lead us to a bombing range near Vung Tau, where we would practise weapons delivery. In Phase III we continued our training with the USAF. This time we would be flying combat missions from the left seat of an A-1E, and the USAF instructor would be strapped into the right seat, watching us and correcting any of our mistakes.'

When Dat completed his training in December 1964, he was ordered to report to the 516th FS at Da Nang AB;

'Our first impressions when we arrived in Da Nang were not that great. Our living quarters consisted of only one large room within a stand-alone building that had no toilet block. Some 20 pilots from various squadrons slept next to each other on old military beds. The toilets were in a different building, and running water was very scarce. Taking a shower was a luxury, and normally we had to obtain water from a well. At night, when heading into town, we had to use cologne to hide our body odour. It was little wonder that most VNAF personnel wanted to stay in Bien Hoa, rather than be assigned to the 516th FS. Being posted to Da Nang was like being posted back in time.'

A-1G 132528 was acquired directly from the US Navy though MAP in May 1965. It was transferred to the USAF in July 1965, along with nine other dual-seat Skyraiders, when demand outpaced supply due to higher than anticipated losses. The aircraft was reacquired by the VNAF four months later and assigned to the 516th FS. This photograph clearly shows where the '2' used to be on the A-1's cowl, the numeral not quite being covered by the 'Flying Tiger' insignia. The large tail number, 32528, in the USAF style, has now been applied in black instead of white. In September 1967 the aircraft was again transferred to the USAF (*Tom Hansen via author's collection*)

Dat described his 'checkout' with the 516th FS at Da Nang;

'With their heavy workload, our seniors had no time to help familiarise us with the area or to better understand the operation of the 516th. We had not yet received any A-1Es, so could not accompany them on their missions. Then, one day, out of the blue, they scheduled us for combat. I have to admit that I was rather worried upon receiving this news. Flying in the mountainous terrain of I Corps was very different to operating over the flat lands of the Mekong Delta. For example, attacking targets at different altitudes in the mountains could affect the accuracy of my bombing. So far I had less than 300 hours of total flying time, and just 30 hours in the A-1, much of it in the right seat of the A-1E whilst being flown by an instructor.'

Dat vividly recalls his first Skyraider combat mission, which he flew on the wing of the squadron commander;

'We were carrying a full load of bombs and rockets. As we lined up on the runway for takeoff, I was focused on maintaining my position in the flight. When it was time for me to go, I released the brakes and quickly pushed the throttle all the way forward as fast as I could. That was a big mistake, as the propeller torque was so strong that the aircraft started veering to the left. I had been cautioned about this before, but this was the first time I had had it happen to me. I tried as hard as I could to make corrections, but because of its heavy load the aeroplane took longer to get airborne.

'Moments after running off the runway the aircraft finally started to lift off. I was more embarrassed than scared. What a humiliation, and I always thought that I was a good pilot! I hoped that my flight leader had not seen anything, but when I looked up I saw him flying right over my head. Soon after taking off, he had made a 180-degree turn over the end of the runway to check and see if I was okay. I assumed that he was mad at me. We continued the mission without further incidents. When we came home and sat down for the de-briefing, I expected to see him bursting with rage and yelling at me, but to my surprise he was very calm. "It was a good flight", he told me. "Your bombing was very accurate and you were able to follow me well in the air. You have a lot of potential, but you better work on your takeoffs". So ended my first combat mission with the 516th FS in the Skyraider.'

A-1H 139664 was photographed in January 1967 sporting unit markings over its camouflage paint. VNAF tail codes from the pre-camouflage era are gone, but the 'Flying Tiger' emblem remains on the cowl. The ordnance load is six 500-lb napalm tanks – note the weapons' tail fuses, visible from this angle. This Skyraider was lost on 15 December 1967 while assigned to the 520th FS (*Robert F Dorr collection*)

Dat described life as a Skyraider pilot in the 516th FS in early 1965;

'Time went by very fast as we were so busy. January quickly rolled into February, and I learned more in that first two months than I had ever learned before. The war rapidly intensified, and we also participated in the bombing of North Vietnam. It was not unusual for each of us to fly two or sometimes three missions a day. We could only take a break during weekends and on rainy days, when we would try and keep the number of missions flown to a minimum. Nevertheless, I remember completing more than 40 missions a month on several occasions. We easily achieved 30 missions a month.

'The price for flying all those sorties was a high casualty rate. In late February and early March, Maj Duong Thieu Hung, deputy wing commander and former squadron commander of the 516th, and 2Lt Nguyen Van Phu were hit during separate missions over North Vietnam. Both bailed out at sea and, fortunately, were rescued. However, on 4 April 1965 Capts Vu Khac Hue and Walter Frank Dreager Jr (the USAF advisor in our squadron) were shot down and killed [near the Dragon's Jaw Bridge, in North Vietnam, during a RESCAP for two downed airmen who had attacked the bridge the previous day]. Capt Hue's aeroplane crashed into the ocean and Capt Dreager's A-1H exploded in midair.'

Capt Walter Frank Draeger Jr was posthumously awarded the Air Force Cross for his actions on this mission. He was one of 14 USAF Skyraider pilots to receive this award during the conflict in Southeast Asia.

Dat described his confidence level after flying Skyraiders for more than a year;

'After several hundred combat missions in South Vietnam I thought I was invincible. I always believed the enemy would never be able to get me. I became more and more careless until on 14 May 1966, whilst leading a flight of three Skyraiders on a mission north of the DMZ along the Ho Chi Minh Trail, I was shot down over the target and the enemy finally got me. It was my 26th, and last, mission over North Vietnam. After almost seven years in the infamous "Hanoi Hilton", having been the only VNAF pilot captured during the bombing of North Vietnam, I was released in March 1973 during Operation *Homecoming*.

'I then spent a few months in South Vietnam, before being sent to the USA for more training. I attended squadron officer school and the academic instructor course in Alabama, before completing instructor pilot training on the T-37 in Texas. Along with all former USAF POWs, I also had my "champagne flight" in a T-38 (call-sign "Freedom 121") at Randolph AFB.

A-1H 139723 from the 516th FS taxis for takeoff at Da Nang in February 1968 with a less than maximum load of Mk 82 LDGP bombs. The many empty outer wing stations indicate that this must have been a period of ordnance rationing, which was pervasive in the later 1960s throughout the VNAF. Note also the absence of the 'Flying Tiger' cowl insignia. No loss record exists for this A-1, although it was not one of the 11 that fled to Thailand in April 1975 (*Robert F Dorr collection*)

Fellow POW and USAF legend Gen Robinson Risner wanted me to remain in the USA so that he could help me rebuild a new life, but I chose to go back to South Vietnam in late 1974 because I did not want to be called a deserter. I started working at the VNAF headquarters in Saigon, but six months later South Vietnam was invaded by the communists. With the help of businessman [and Presidential candidate] Ross Perot, I was able to get all the members of my family out of the country. This happened in April 1975, just a week or so before the fall of South Vietnam.

'As a two-time loser, I decided to leave Vietnam for good! The first time was in 1954, when the communists took over North Vietnam (I was born in Hanoi), and the second time was in 1975, when South Vietnam fell to the communists.'

The 516th FS had 14 pilots killed or listed as MIA during the five years it flew the A-1 – a total of 23 Skyraiders were lost. The unit's heaviest year for attrition was 1965, when it lost seven A-1s and had five pilots killed or listed as MIA. 1965 was also the highest Skyraider loss year for the VNAF, which had no fewer than 43 A-1s destroyed.

518th FS

Formed in October 1963 at Bien Hoa as the second VNAF A-1 squadron, the 518th FS initially borrowed Skyraiders from the 514th before receiving its own fleet of A-1Hs. One of the unit's first COs was Maj Nguyen Quoc Thanh, and many of his pilots were products of the 34th TG and VA-152

American advisor Capt Mark Diebolt poses with 518th FS A-1H 137587 before a mission from Bien Hoa AB in 1964. His ordnance load for this sortie was two M65 1000-lb GP bombs, 12 M57 250-lb GP bombs and, of course, 800 rounds of 20 mm ammunition. This aircraft was a combat loss on 5 February 1965 (*Mark Diebolt*)

training programme. As previously mentioned, Maj Thanh left the 518th for the 83rd SAG at the request of Col Ky in late 1964.

The 518th flew similar missions to the other VNAF A-1 units during the conflict, being based at Bien Hoa throughout its 12-year existence. The squadron was heavily involved in repelling the NVA from South Vietnamese soil following the Easter Invasion of 30 March 1972, 20 of its A-1s being hastily deployed to Da Nang AB to provide the embattled ARVN with CAS. VNAF HQ gave the 518th just two hours to complete preparations for the week-long deployment.

Squadron pilot 1Lt Nguyen Lanh described the events that unfolded after the unit's arrival at Da Nang;

'Nobody knew what the target was going to be until we gathered for a mission briefing. Typically for this time of year, the weather was not good. The forecast called for ceilings of around 1000 ft, with rain showers for the entire week. The NVA had planned well, hoping that the poor weather would keep the VNAF on the ground.

'The 516th FS and its A-37s was the other force available for combat from Da Nang during the coming few days.

'Intelligence briefed that the NVA had crossed the DMZ in division strength, with armour, and to date had advanced to a point just northwest of Dong Ha, about 200 kilometres from Da Nang. The advancing column, led by armoured vehicles, was travelling along Highway 1, and it was threatening to cross the river south of Dong Ha.'

The weather on 5 April was dominated by a low overcast that did not clear until around 1500 hrs. Lanh continued;

'All the aircraft were loaded and ready to go. I was selected to be leader of the first two-ship of A-1s into the area, each Skyraider carrying 12 Mk 82s. We contacted our FAC, who was in an L-19. We were now about five nautical miles south of Dong Ha, and I could see the Highway 1 bridge

Capt Tho of the 518th FS smiles for USAF Capt Herb Tidwell, who took this photograph just before their mission from Bien Hoa in 1969. The ordnance load is six Mk 82 HDGP Snakeyes. The latter had four folded fins that snapped open after release, greatly reducing the speed of the weapon so as to increase the separation distance of the aircraft from the bomb detonation on impact. This was particularly useful when working beneath a low cloud ceiling (*Herb Tidwell*)

This A-1H from the 518th FS carries a substantial load of six M1A frag cluster bombs, six Mk 82 LDGP bombs and two M117 GP bombs. Each of the adjacent aircraft is loaded with this same ordnance, indicating no bomb shortages during this period. 137502 was lost on 8 July 1972 (*Norm Taylor via Robert F Dorr*)

crossing the Mieu Giang River just north of the town. On the north side of the bridge I spotted the armoured column that was heading south. The FAC cleared us to attack. I began attacking the front of the column while my wingman targeted the rear. As I was pulling off from my second pass, I felt and heard a loud explosion. It was the bridge being demolished so the tanks could not cross. I also observed black puffs of smoke in the sky from AAA.

'After releasing all of our ordnance we departed the area, thus allowing other pilots from our squadron to target the column.'

The attacks by the 518th FS continued until dusk, as the armoured vehicles that had survived these strikes had a difficult time getting off the road and under cover because of the muddy rice paddies that ran along either side of Highway 1. This in turn made them easy targets for the A-1 pilots, all of whom returned safely in high spirits following their first day of combat from Da Nang AB.

'The weather continued to be good on 6 April', Lanh recalled. 'Overnight, the NVA had frantically moved its remaining tanks under the cover of trees in the hope that they wouldn't be detected by the FAC. The latter had little difficulty finding them the following morning, however, my flight being over the target area at 0830 hrs with orders to destroy more tanks. The FAC had found four hidden under a tree near the riverbank east of Highway 1 and one more to the west of this position. We were able to destroy these tanks without much difficulty. After landing, I discovered that my aeroplane had been hit by a single 12.7 mm round in the right wheel well cover.'

On 7 April the weather remained good, allowing the pilots of the 518th FS to continue in their hunt for tanks. By then the remaining NVA armour was moving west in an attempt to find a river crossing so that they could then continue south toward Quang Tri and Da Nang. The 518th FS lost two A-1s on this day and Capt Phan Quang Tuan was killed. Maj Hung was the other pilot shot down, as Lanh explained;

'Our aeroplanes continued to destroy tanks to the west and northwest of Dong Ha. During one such attack Maj Hung's A-1 was hit by groundfire shortly after he had destroyed several tanks. Flying his aircraft away from the target area, Hung bailed out after his Skyraider caught fire and started losing altitude. As he steered his 'chute towards an area

63

A-1H 139746 nears the runway at Bien Hoa upon its return from a mission in the summer of 1972. By this stage in the conflict there were more important things to be concerned about than the appearance of aircraft, and this one is looking a little worn. There is no record of loss for 139746 (*Bill Stevens*)

southeast of Dong Ha, soldiers from the NVA took several shots at him. Luckily for Hung he was eventually rescued by friendly troops.'

The weather deteriorated on the 8th, keeping the 518th FS grounded for the day. Despite continuing poor conditions, the battle resumed on 9 April, as Lanh recalled;

'The weather en route to the target was very bad, with low cloud ceilings and rain. Had this been a "normal mission" we would have turned back, but nothing about the flying during the Easter Invasion was normal. Flying at an altitude of less than 1000 ft, we followed the coastline until we finally found better weather. We then climbed up to the base of the clouds. A few minutes later the FAC informed us that there were about 20 tanks threatening a remote ARVN base west of Dong Ha. We were again carrying Mk 82s, and with the low clouds anti-tank rockets would have been better.

'As we approached, we could see the tanks trying to reverse course to the west. We dropped all our ordnance in one pass in the hope of catching them in the open. As we reversed course back to the east, we flew through a large barrage of AAA before reaching the safety of the clouds. My wingman rejoined and we headed back to Da Nang.'

The remaining flights from the 518th that targeted the same tanks also encountered heavy AAA, prompting some pilots to remark that they had never seen such a high concentration of flak before. The third flight to attack was led by Capt Tran The Vinh, who, as he released his bombs and then began to strafe the armoured vehicles, was shot down and killed.

The following day the 514th FS from Bien Hoa replaced the 518th at Da Nang. During the unit's one-week deployment, its men had helped the ARVN repel the NVA offensive. The Skyraiders of the 518th FS had flown 52 missions and dropped 78 tons of bombs on the enemy. Intelligence reports confirmed that Capt Vinh had destroyed 21 tanks prior to his death, while 1Lt Nguyen Lanh had knocked out 17 tanks and Capt Truong Phung a total of 16 tanks. The price for this success was a high one, however, as the 518th lost three Skyraiders and had two pilots killed.

By April 1975 the 518th FS was one of only two squadrons in the VNAF still flying the venerable A-1. One of the last pilots to serve with the unit was 2Lt Nguyen Van Chuyen, who had completed his Skyraider training at Hurlburt Field in 1972. He subsequently flew with the 518th for his entire three-year VNAF career, from June 1972 to his final mission on 24 April 1975. Chuyen described his life as an A-1 pilot with the unit at this time;

'During my three years with the 518th I was usually scheduled to fly for two days and then have a day off. I usually flew two missions during the day and one at night. Sometimes I flew more missions, but that was not the norm. Our primary task was to provide CAS when our troops and the enemy were very close. Most of my missions were flown over South Vietnam.'

Chuyen described the survival equipment he flew with;

'VNAF pilots were equipped with a small 0.38-cal Smith & Wesson revolver for protection. In my survival vest, besides a flare gun, a compass, a strobe light and an emergency radio, I had packed a small and powerful hand grenade for use, just in case. In the heat of the battle, captured VNAF pilots were usually tortured and killed in the most horrible ways. US pilots would be treated more fairly because they could be used as bargaining chips with the American government. A captured VNAF pilot was worthless to the communists.'

Chuyen lived through the chaotic last days of the VNAF, and South Vietnam, in April 1975;

'Even at this late stage in the conflict I did not realise that South Vietnam was falling. We had continued to fly countless missions from Bien Hoa in support of our ground troops until we were ordered to evacuate the base and head to Tan Son Nhut on 24 April. The runway was jammed when we tried to depart, so we were directed to use the taxiway for takeoff instead. My flight leader, 1Lt Loc Huu Pham, veered to the right during his takeoff roll and, despite his best efforts, was going off the taxiway. He extracted just as he was leaving the taxiway. I watched as the Yankee system pulled him out and gave him a 'chute when he was just 50 ft off the ground. I was sure that he was dead. I took off over the top of his wreckage. Amazingly, Loc survived the crash, paid a motorcyclist to take him to Tan Son Nhut and joined me that evening!

'There was no clear communication from commanders to the rank and file of the squadron regarding the pending collapse of the country. I never knew, or thought, Saigon and South Vietnam were ever going to fall. In many cases, commanders abandoned the lower ranking personnel, who were left to fend for themselves. When my family was evacuated to Tan Son Nhut from Bien Hoa we had to leave all our personal belongings behind. Shortly after we had left the latter base, and just prior to communist troops seizing it from the ARVN, my wife, Nguyen T Ngoc-Thuy, risked her life by single-handedly going back to our room at the Base Officers' Quarters to retrieve many of our irreplaceable photographs.

'This was a horrifying period not just for my wife and children but for me too, since we did not have any bomb shelters near the temporary quarters where we were staying – a wooden table would have offered us no protection whatsoever had we been hit by a shell. Tan Son Nhut AB was shelled by 130 mm field guns from 0400 hrs to 0900 hrs on 29 April. There was widespread destruction as aeroplanes and buildings were set ablaze. The shelling also caused many deaths. We dodged fires and rocket craters, as well as shells as they whizzed overhead, during our escape.

'Two hours after we had survived the shelling, my wife and I, our two-month-old son and my five-year-old brother escaped to U-Tapao RTAFB in a VNAF C-119 transport aircraft. Most of the surviving pilots from the 518th, and their families, were also on that aeroplane.'

The departure of the C-119 for Thailand marked the end of the 518th FS's long association with the A-1. During its nine years of combat operations the unit had suffered the loss of 40 Skyraiders, which had resulted in 18 pilots being either killed or listed as MIA.

520th FS

The last of the original quartet of A-1 units to be formed by the VNAF, the 520th FS received its first Skyraiders in June 1964 as more aircraft arrived in South Vietnam through MAP. The squadron was based at Bien Hoa, making it the fifth A-1 unit (three VNAF and two USAF squadrons) to operate from here at this time. The 520th would subsequently move to the new air base at Binh Thuy, near Can Tho, in August 1965, this location giving the unit much better coverage of Military Region IV – the delta area south of Saigon.

The 520th FS had begun staging out of Binh Thuy in early 1965, pilots landing there after flying out of Bien Hoa in the morning for their first mission. Having had their A-1s rearmed and refuelled with pre-positioned ordnance and fuel, pilots would conclude their next strike sortie with recovery back at Bien Hoa. Then lacking sufficiently robust security to ward off nocturnal attacks by the VC, Binh Thuy remained a day-only base until the improvement of its facilities was completed in August 1965. Co-located with the 520th FS was its parent unit, the VNAF's 74th TW.

As with other VNAF Skyraider units, the 520th had USAF advisors during the early years of its existence. One such individual was 1Lt Herb Meyr who flew with the unit both at Bien Hoa and Binh Thuy in 1965-66. The advisors were not there to instruct or to lead missions, but more to monitor the unit's operation, and to make sure that the VNAF was getting what it needed it terms of support from the USAF.

An unidentified VNAF Skyraider pilot poses in front of A-1H 135279 at Binh Thuy AB in November 1965. This aircraft shows the original Panther cowl design that was subsequently changed in mid-1966. Note the matching patch on the pilot's K2B flightsuit. The small letter 'v' on the landing gear 'kneecap' was a squadron marking applied to all 520th FS Skyraiders, with a variety of other, larger, letters following (*Herb Meyr*)

Standing in stark contrast with the rest of the 520th FS Skyraider fleet, these three colourful A-1s were photographed on the Binh Thuy ramp in September 1966. Both the A-1Hs shown here had been added to the VNAF Skyraider fleet in the spring of 1965, having each completed around 3600 flying hours in service with the US Navy since they had came off the Douglas assembly line in the mid-1950s (*Herb Meyr*)

Meyr initially told the author about his conversion onto the Skyraider at Hurlburt Field in 1965;

'At first we were told that we would get our Skyraider checkouts from the US Navy, but that never happened. When we showed up at Hurlburt Field it seemed as if they were unaware we were coming.'

Meyr, who was one of six advisors bound for Vietnam, received a fast checkout and was on his way in less than two months. Once in-theatre, one of his early mission proved to be particularly interesting. There was growing evidence that the VC were being re-supplied by sea along the coast of the Gulf of Thailand. Up until that time none of the vessels involved had been interdicted, but that was about to change. Word was received by the squadron late one afternoon that there was a large 120-ft 100-ton freighter stationary off the coast of the Ca Mau Peninsula. It had been pursued by a US Coast Guard cutter and had run aground on the beach about 100 nautical miles southwest of Binh Thuy.

With no flare ship available for a night air strike, the 520th FS's operations officer, Capt Nguyen Van Truong, asked Meyr if there was a way to drop flares from the A-1. He in turn spoke with the squadron's USAF maintenance advisor NCO, who told him that flares could be loaded in the 'blue room' and dropped manually by a crewman out of the 'trap door' – officially the drift signal chute. Having checked the size of the opening to confirm that an LUU-2 flare would indeed pass through it, 520th FS personnel loaded the 'blue room' of an A-1E with flares. The USAF NCO volunteered to ride in the back and drop the flares out of the chute, activating them by holding onto to the flare's firing lanyard as it fell down the chute.

Once Truong had received word of the suitability of the LUU-2, he formulated a plan for a night strike on the stranded ship. Truong would lead two other A-1Hs in the attack, with Meyr flying as No 4 in the A-1E flare ship. The flight took off well after dark and headed to the target area, where Meyr broke away from the formation and flew along the shoreline at about 5000 ft. He then told the NCO in the 'blue room' to drop a string of flares. Once ignited, the illuminated flares revealed many VC-manned small boats being used to transport weapons from the freighter onto the beach.

Truong and the other two A-1 pilots bombed and strafed the enemy personnel and weapons on the beach, while boats fleeing the area were also hit. Meyr kept the target area illuminated throughout this time, allowing his VNAF counterparts to also spot the ship itself, motionless just off the coast. Truong and his wingmen duly attacked the vessel,

but could not sink it. When they departed the area there were fires and secondary explosions all along on the beach. Early the next morning another three-aircraft flight from the 520th attacked the ship, and this time one of the VNAF pilots dropped a 500-lb bomb down its funnel. The subsequent explosion split the vessel in two.

A-1H 137519 flies on 1Lt Herb Meyr's wing following a CAS mission in Military Region IV in February 1966. Showing clear signs of wear, the markings on this Skyraider are looking a little tired. 137519 was lost on 20 August 1966 (*Herb Meyr*)

RESCUE IN THE DELTA

1Lt Duong Thieu Chi was one of the most experienced A-1 pilots in the VNAF, flying around 2500 missions in the aircraft – many of these were completed whilst serving with the 520th FS. He was also one of only a handful of South Vietnamese pilots to have been awarded the US Distinguished Flying Cross, the medal being presented to Chi after he participated in a CAS mission in support of a US Army Special Forces camp. The citation that accompanied the medal noted that his actions during this mission were directly responsible for the saving of 18 American lives.

In 1967 it was Chi's turn to be saved after he took off in one of three 520th FS A-1s sent aloft on a 'hot-scramble' mission. With him in 'Jellyfish' flight were Lt Thai and Maj Davis Glass (an American advisor), the three pilots heading southwest toward the Ca-Mau Peninsula, in the Gulf of Thailand, where a full battalion of NVA troops was threatening to overrun the company-sized local defence force in the Quan-Long district. Their flight had plenty of firepower, the three Skyraiders being loaded with GP bombs, CBUs and napalm. Chi, whose A-1 carried 12 CBU-14s and two 750-lb napalm tanks on the stub pylons, explains what happened next;

'The FAC briefed us when we were about five minutes away from the target. He told us that this would be an easy target for us to recognise – a large group of bad guys in black pyjamas in the middle of a rice paddy. The FAC put in a smoke canister and we went to work. Earlier, he had warned us about ground fire – mostly AK-47s, but also some heavier 12.7 mm AAA. I dropped napalm on my first pass and then re-attacked with CBUs on my next four passes. As I pulled off on my final pass, my aeroplane wanted to go right even though I was banking left. I was able to climb to about 1500 ft when the A-1 went out of control. I reached for the Yankee extraction handle and was jerked out of the Skyraider.'

1Lt Duong Thieu Chi poses proudly with his A-1H before a mission with the 520th FS. Chi, who flew around 2500 combat missions in the Skyraider, was one of the few VNAF pilots to have earned the US Distinguished Flying Cross. He received this decoration after providing CAS for a US Special Forces camp that was threatened with being overrun. Chi was directly responsible for saving 18 American lives during the course of this mission (*Duong Thieu Chi*)

At first, Chi found it very quiet as he drifted down in his 'chute. 'I quickly realised that I could barely breathe. I discovered that the chest-strap of my parachute harness was pressing against my throat, so I pulled it down for relief. Suddenly, I heard the sound of automatic weapons fire and saw tracers coming up at me as I hung in my 'chute. I desperately wanted to get to the ground, but my relatively light weight caused a slow descent rate. Finally, having reached the ground, I made a rescue call on my radio'.

The FAC answered, and he told Chi that he had instructed the local defence force to come to his rescue. Chi saw the Skyraiders from his flight making passes nearby, and he could also hear the ground fire being shot at them. Anxious to move away from where he had landed in his 'chute, Chi slogged his way through the wet rice paddy for a few hundred metres until he stopped at the edge of a canal that was too wide for him to cross.

It was getting dark and he needed to find cover. Chi could hear that there were NVA near him, so he called his flight with his position. He dug into the bank of the canal and asked his flight to strafe on top of his location where the AK-47 fire was coming from. 'After two strafing passes, a couple of palm trees with coconuts and banana tree branches came crashing down around me and the AK-47s were quiet', Chi recalled. 'It was very scary to be at the receiving end of the "twenty-mike-mike" strafing'.

A short while later Chi's radio came alive again. '"Jellyfish 2", the friendlies are 500 metres from you and are asking for a flare'. Chi figured that the enemy was closer than that so he waited. Soon he heard voices, speaking Vietnamese, nearby. They then said in English, 'You okay? You okay?' Chi replied in Vietnamese, 'I am not an American, I am a Vietnamese from the Vietnamese Air Force'. Chi heard the troops talking amongst themselves, saying 'He is an American speaking Vietnamese. Viets do not fly aircraft'. By then Chi had had enough, and he said sternly, 'Let me talk to your commander. My name is Lt Duong from the 520th FS'. The confusion as to his identity was quickly solved.

Soon after he had been helped back to friendly territory by his rescuers, Chi heard the sound of an approaching helicopter. As it slowed and landed next to him, he scrambled aboard and was flown back to Binh Thuy. Upon his arrival home Chi was greeted by the wing commander and many of the pilots from the 520th FS.

The next day Chi was flown back to where he was shot down in the Quan-Long district in a U-17, and he met with the local ARVN commander and his men. Whilst there, he also wanted to show both the troops that had rescued him and local villagers that there was such a thing as the VNAF, manned by Vietnamese pilots. The district commander told Chi, 'They didn't really believe us last night when we told them that you were Vietnamese. Over the years they have seen a few downed pilots, but they were all Americans. On other occasions they have had flights in

1Lt Duong Thieu Chi of the 520th FS explains his use of the RT-10 survival radio and signal flare following his shoot down and subsequent rescue in 1967. Maj Davis Glass, the American advisor to the squadron, 22nd TASS FAC Capt Tomas Goronowski and Chi's flight leader 1Lt Thuy Thai look on (*Duong Thieu Chi*)

transport aeroplanes that were also American. They had never heard of the Vietnamese Air Force'.

Chi's A-1 was just one of 17 Skyraiders lost by the 520th FS during its time operating the aircraft, initially from Bien Hoa and then Binh Thuy. Ten pilots were either killed or listed as MIA. Among the men lost was American advisor Maj William Richardson Jr, who was killed on 2 April 1966 whilst strafing a target in Vinh Long province, south of Saigon.

The 520th replaced its A-1s with A-37s in 1969, retaining these aircraft until the annihilation of the VNAF in April 1975.

524th FS

Another A-1 unit that was destined to swap its A-1s for A-37s, the 524th FS flew Skyraiders at Nha Trang AB from September 1965 through to early 1969. Initially formed with T-28s in 1961, the squadron received A-1s so that it could help the VNAF fill the CAS coverage gap that existed in eastern Military Regions II and III.

VNAF pilot Maj Son Thanh Luu flew Skyraiders with the 524th from 1966 until the unit switched to the A-37. Having graduated from T-28 training at Randolph AFB in 1965, he then attended 'Skyraider school' at Hurlburt Field for six months in 1966 before joining the 524th;

'During my time with the squadron we always had a detachment at Pleiku AB – about half the unit would operate from there, with the other half at Nha Trang. We would spend two weeks at a time at each location. Our missions were normally CAS, working with a VNAF FAC. Early on we carried 12 Mk 81s, but from the Tet Offensive onwards we carried a mixed load of four Mk 81s and four Mk 82s. The targets we attacked during Tet were very close, but we also flew further afield to attack enemy

At least two American advisors to the 524th FS are seen here as they enjoy food and drink at a 'party-like' setting at Binh Thuy AB in 1966 (*Richard Foreman*)

staging areas. Towards the end of my time with the 524th FS we would only carry six Mk 82s on each sortie. By then we were running low of bombs, and also spare parts for our A-1s. We were subsequently grounded through a lack of fuel in late 1968.'

1Lt Richard Foreman was a USAF advisor to the 524th FS at Nha Trang in 1965-66. Here, he recalls his arrival in Vietnam;

'After a couple of days in processing, I was to meet a VNAF pilot at Tan Son Nhut for a ride to Nha Trang in an A-1E. I was in the right seat, and in the back were five or six Vietnamese with their belongings, including a few chickens. It was supposed to be a one hour flight, but due to the weather, it took a little longer.'

As the VNAF pilot began to circumnavigate some rain showers, Foreman felt a little vulnerable due to his complete lack of familiarity with his surroundings. 'We dropped down low to get under some rain clouds and I hoped the terrain remained flat. We finally arrived at Nha Trang by hitting the coast and turning left'.

Maintenance personnel work on A-1H 139637 at Nha Trang AB in 1966. The Thien Loi emblem on the cowl means 'God of Thunder'. There is no record of loss for this aircraft (*Richard Foreman*)

American advisor Capt Richard Foreman pre-flights the ordnance on his A-1 in 1966 at Nha Trang AB. Note the single bomb lug on the bottom of the M64 500-lb GP bomb, thus making it useable on aircraft that used a one-lug suspension system (*Richard Foreman*)

Foreman was part of a squadron deployment to Pleiku in 1966, and during his time at the base he had met an American intelligence officer who was assigned to the 14th ACW that supported the 1st ACS at Pleiku. He had asked Foreman if he could go out on a mission with him, to which the A-1 pilot replied, 'Sure, grab your gear'.

The targets at that time were not far from Pleiku, as Foreman recalled;

'We switched from tower frequency after takeoff, and I was talking to the FAC almost immediately. I told my passenger to hang on as I set up my switches and rolled in for my first pass. I tended to jink a lot in case of AAA, and since the Skyraider tended to fly a bit uncoordinated due to the torque, and with my abrupt manoeuvring, the next thing I knew my right-seater had his helmet off and he was puking in it. I cracked the canopy back just a bit to freshen the air and continued with a couple more passes.'

After they finished the strike, Foreman looked over to see how his passenger was doing;

'His eyes were glazed over and his head was down on his chest. After we landed the groundcrew and I had to help him out of the aeroplane. I subsequently heard that he had been admitted to hospital for a few days, but found out later that he was okay. I bet he thought twice before asking to go flying again.'

HUNG NAPALM

Maj Son related a story to the author about a particularly dangerous situation that he said 'scared him to death';

'I will never forget one mission when I was carrying six napalm tanks. We always flew a curved approach to the target so as to reduce the chances of getting hit by ground fire. My plan after dropping my ordnance was to pull off to the left, away from the highest threat. I set up the switches to drop all the napalm on one pass, but just after I released the napalm the aircraft rolled violently to the right. I thought I had been hit, but when I looked out I saw that the napalm beneath the right wing had failed to release. As I struggled to keep the aircraft out of the trees I used lots of

A-1G 134976 sits in a sandbag revetment in 1966 at Da Nang, parked next to a Skyraider from the resident 516th FS. Note the *FWD* arrow pointing to the rear of the napalm – clearly this 'instruction' was a suggestion only! 134976 was lost on 12 February 1968 while assigned to the 516th FS (*Tom Hanson via author's collection*)

left rudder to level the wings and eventually climb out. I was finally able to get the napalm off with the manual release system in our free fire zone near Nha Trang. When the aircraft flipped over I really thought I was going to die.'

On another occasion, while returning from a mission, Son heard calls on his FM radio that indicated a ground unit was lost. He quickly determined that a platoon was isolated from its main group and had no idea which way to go. The lost platoon's lieutenant had been killed in a firefight with the VC, and although the remaining troops were now disengaged from the enemy, they were panicked and completely disoriented. The heavy jungle canopy hid the sun in the cloudy sky.

Son contacted the unit's HQ via his FM radio and soon found their location. He then radioed the lost platoon and tried to calm them down. Once they understood that this might be their salvation, they followed his instructions. Son told them to 'pop a smoke so I can locate you'. Soon the wisps of coloured smoke drifted up through the jungle canopy. He then said, 'I am going to fly over you in the direction you should go. I will rock my wings when I am above your position'. Son descended to treetop height and lined up with the location of the HQ. Rocking his wings as he flew over the platoon, he radioed, 'I am heading towards your headquarters, follow my direction'. Son later learned that the lost platoon was indeed reunited with its HQ.

The 524th FS operated Skyraiders at Nha Trang AB for four years from 1965 though to early 1969. During that period it lost 12 A-1s and had nine pilots either killed or listed as MIA. Half of the aircraft losses and five of the casualties occurred in 1966, the squadron's first full year of operations.

FINAL SKYRAIDER UNITS

Although the arrival of A-37s in South Vietnam in increasing numbers from late 1968 allowed the VNAF to convert three of its A-1 units to the Cessna attack aircraft, the Skyraider continued to play a key role in supporting the ARVN through to the communist invasion of April 1975. USAF A-1s also remained active in the SAR role until they were finally withdrawn in late 1972, the few surviving examples being passed on to the VNAF.

Although the Dragonfly was seen as the future light attack platform for the South Vietnamese, proof that there was still a role for the venerable A-1 in-theatre came in 1970 when the 530th FS became the last Skyraider squadron to form within the VNAF. Based at Pleiku, the nucleus of the unit was provided by an A-1 detachment from the 524th FS that had operated from the base until the squadron had converted to the A-37 in early 1969. The Skyraider's presence at Pleiku had been further reduced in November of that year when the USAF's 6th SOS, which had flown from the base since early 1968, was inactivated. The ARVN was anxious to keep a strong CAS presence in Military Region II, however, so the 530th FS was formed in 1970 with surplus A-1s following the conversion of two units to the A-37.

Although the squadron boasted a highly experienced leadership cadre (CO, vice commander and operations officer), most of its pilots were young aviators who had been trained at Hurlburt Field within the previous year. The number of experienced A-1 pilots in the VNAF had been significantly reduced following their conversion onto the A-37 at Da Nang, Nha Trang and Bin Thuy.

As with other VNAF Skyraider squadrons, the normal duty cycle within the 530th FS was two days on, one day off. That is to say pilots would fly for two days and perform other squadron duties every third day. Missions were flown mostly during daylight hours and rarely at night. Although the

The pilot of A-1H 134494 of the 530th FS joins other flight members as they hold short of the runway at Pleiku in 1971. Each Skyraider is loaded with six Mk 82s – a modest load for the aircraft, but a sign that there was already a shortage of munitions. Note the tailhook on 134494, indicating that it was a transfer from US stocks. Also note the USAF-style tail number, 'AF 34 494'. In fact this aircraft had been transferred to the VNAF in early 1971, only to be lost on 15 February 1973 (*Peter Bird*)

1Lt Pham Minh Xuan poses on the wing of his A-1 prior to flying a mission in 1971. Note the close detail of the 'production' 'Daisy Cutter' fuse extenders. The nose fuse at the end of the extender gave this weapon dual fuse redundancy. Clearly visible is the fuse arming wire that went through the fuse 'propeller' to be held by a fahnestock clip. When the bomb left the aircraft, the wire (retained by the aircraft) pulled out of the fuse propeller, allowing the latter to spin until it armed the weapon (*Pham Xuan*)

addition of the BOBS (beacon-only bombing system) allowed bombs to be dropped in either bad weather and/or at night, still the vast majority of A-1 sorties were performed during the day.

One such mission saw the 530th called on to support a fire support base (FSB) that was being overrun by the enemy. 'Jupiter 11', a flight of two Skyraiders flown by Maj Thanh and his wingman, 1Lt Pham Minh Xuan, were scrambled from Pleiku after the call had come in from FSB 'Charlie' that it needed help fast. The famed Red Berets of the ARVN's 11th Airborne Battalion were just holding on in the face of stiff opposition from a larger enemy force. 'We were airborne within ten minutes of the scramble notice being received', Pham recalled. 'My leader, Maj Thanh, was flying an A-1E loaded with six Mk 82s, and I had six cans of 500-lb napalm on my A-1H. We each had a full load of 20 mm ammunition'.

The target was less than 100 nautical miles north of Pleiku, so 'Jupiter 11' was soon over the FSB. The FAC was orbiting nearby, and he briefed the 'Jupiters' on the situation. They were instructed to monitor FM radio channel 47.0 for possible information from the Red Berets on the ground. The plan was for 'Jupiter 11' to drop his bombs first, followed by 'Jupiter 12' with his napalm. After Thanh was finished with his attack, the ground team came on the radio. Pham described what happened next;

'As soon as the FAC gave me my instructions, I heard the Red Berets say that they were being overrun by the enemy – they were coming in human-wave attacks across the perimeter of FSB "Charlie". The enemy was coming up the hill from the south, so I was instructed to drop my napalm no closer than the perimeter of the FSB. My first pass was a little long, so I manoeuvred for my second run. This was much better than the first one, and the Red Berets were yelling for more of the same. My last pass was a repeat of this heading, which turned out to be a big mistake. I felt and heard enemy fire hit the front of my A-1 as I pulled off target.'

Pham climbed as hard as he could for altitude, checking his engine instruments at the same time while starting a turn toward Dak To airfield, which was only a short distance away;

'I noticed that the CHT [cylinder head temperature] was in the red and the engine was running rough, so I pulled the throttle back a bit. I was at about 3000 ft above the ground, and I could no longer maintain altitude, so I pushed the throttle up again. I was able to level off, but I could now see smoke and smelled hydraulic fluid.

'There were two helicopters on the runway at Dak To, so Thanh buzzed them with his gear and flaps down and they got the message and cleared the area. I slid back the canopy to get rid of the smoke, and that helped a lot. The gear would not come down, so I prepared for a gear up landing. I held the aircraft at 90 knots until I flared for landing, and came down with a thud. I was surprised at how quickly the aircraft stopped. I jumped out of the A-1 as fast as I could just in case it caught fire. Later, I had a good look at the aircraft, and discovered several holes in the front of the engine that had been made by 12.7 mm AAA. I had had a lucky escape, as had the Red Berets at FSB Charlie.'

VALOUR BEYOND THE COCKPIT

Many flying stories begin when the pilot takes off, en route to some dangerous target far behind enemy lines. This one commenced when two men were shot down in the midst of the enemy. Neither knew the other, but they were soon to become united in a struggle for survival.

Capt Bill Reeder was a US Army AH-1G Cobra pilot supporting the ARVN Ranger outpost at Ben when he was downed by enemy fire on 9 May 1972. His co-pilot/gunner, Lt Tim Conry, died from his injuries

Two 530th FS A-1Hs, both transfers from the USAF, await clearance for takeoff at Pleiku. Still wearing their USAF-style tail markings (minus the two letter Air Force code), these Skyraiders formed the core of the 530th fleet. A-1H 139779 and A-1J 142014 were lost on 27 May 1972 and 30 September 1971, respectively (*Peter Bird*)

Four pilots from the 530th FS at Pleiku show their individuality by wearing four different flight suits. As for me, I definitely would not want to be wearing orange in a combat zone! (*Pham Xuan*)

shortly after the helicopter had crashed. Earlier, he and Reeder had witnessed the downing of an A-1 Skyraider near Polei Klang, but they had been denied permission to attempt to rescue the pilot. The latter, Lt Nguyen Dinh Xanh of the 530th FS, had been supporting ARVN forces at Polei Klang, an outpost west of Kontum near the Cambodian border, when his A-1 was hit by AAA.

'I had a badly broken back, burns on the back of my neck, a piece of shell fragment sticking out of my ankle and superficial wounds on my head and face', Reeder recalled. 'I was in the midst of many hundreds of attacking enemy soldiers'.

After evading the enemy for three days, Reeder was captured and herded to a prison camp carved out of the jungle just inside Cambodia. 'There were South Vietnamese military [prisoners], there were indigenous mountain people referred to as Montagnards who had allied with US Special Forces and there were two Americans, myself and another helicopter pilot, Wayne Finch, captured a month earlier', Reeder explained. 'There were at least 200 prisoners altogether'.

Xanh had also been captured following his shoot down on 9 April 1972. He too had been force-marched through the jungle to this very same camp. Reeder described his meeting with Xanh on 2 July 1972, nearly three months after he had been captured;

'My weight went from around 190 pounds to somewhere around 120 in just a few weeks. I was skin hanging on bone, with a beard that grew very long over time. I did not shave for more than five months. I received no medical attention at all, and no one fared any better than me. One day I was taken outside my cage and lined up with a group of prisoners. There were about 25 South Vietnamese, as well as Wayne and myself. I would soon learn that one of our group was a pilot who had been shot down on the same day as me in an A-1 Skyraider at Polei Klang – the very same Vietnamese pilot I had been denied the chance of rescuing. His name was Lt Xanh.'

The group was told by one of their guards that they would be taken to an improved camp where they would receive medical treatment. 'You all should try hard to make it', the guard told them. 'It should only take about 11 days'. Reeder described his mindset as they set off down the trail;

'If you did not continue to march, you would die. In normal life you have to take some overt action in order to die. You have to kill yourself. As a prisoner of war, under these circumstances, that truth is reversed. You have to reach deep within yourself and struggle each day to stay alive. Dying is easy. Just relax, give up and peacefully surrender, and you will die. Many did. They died in that first jungle prison camp, and they died along the trail. Some would complete a day's journey and then lie down to die. Others collapsed on the trail and could not continue.'

The journey to the next camp lasted three months, the march covering several hundred miles until it finally ended in Hanoi. 'It was a nightmare, a horrid soul wrenching nightmare', Reeder remembered. 'Every step, every day wracked my body with pain. My infections became worse and disease settled in me. I was near death. The pain kept my face contorted and a cry shrieking within every corner of my consciousness, pain that was burning a blackened scar deep into the centre of my very being. And there was Lt Xanh, suffering badly himself, but always encouraging me, always helping as he could'.

Lt Xanh became a part of Reeder's life at this moment. 'On the worst day of my life I fought so very hard. I faltered. I dug deeper. I staggered on. I faltered again, and I struggled more, and I reached deeper yet, and I prayed for more strength. And I collapsed, and I got up and moved along, and I collapsed again, and again. I fought, fought with all I had in my body, my heart and my soul. And I collapsed, and I could not get up. I could not will myself up. I was at the end of my life. And the enemy came.

'The guard looked down on me. He ordered me up. He yelled at me. I could not. I was done. And then there was Xanh, looking worried, bending toward me, the guard yelling to discourage his effort. He persisted in moving to help me. The guard yelled louder. Xanh's face was set with determination, and in spite of whatever threats the guard was screaming, he pulled me up onto his frail, weak back, pulled my arms around his neck and clasped my wrists together. He then pulled me along with my feet dragging on the ground behind him. Xanh dragged me along for the rest of that day. Occasionally, he was briefly relieved by another prisoner, but it was Xanh who carried the burden that day. It was Xanh who lifted me from death, at great risk to his own life, and carried me, and cared for me, until we completed that long day's journey'.

Skyraiders destined for the 6th ACS are parked side-by-side at the small US Army airfield at Cam Ranh Bay in 1968. Maintenance crews have been working furiously to remove the protective coating that was applied to keep the salt spray off the aircraft during their voyage across the Pacific Ocean. Cam Ranh Bay was used from 1968 onward as the arrival point for most of the A-1H/Js that arrived in-theatre from the USA (*Rob Cole*)

The following morning Reeder's ordeal was not over. Despite the glimmer of hope provided by the previous day's miracle, he fell from a log and lay in a shallow river. This time Xanh was forbidden to help him, he and the other prisoners being marched away at gunpoint. 'They were marched away with the rest of our prisoner group. I never saw Xanh again', Reeder explained.

However, for some reason his captors decided to give Reeder penicillin injections to treat his massive infections and, after a time, he was able to stand, and even walk again. 'I was put back on the trail, this time travelling with groups of North Vietnamese soldiers moving north, and accompanied by my own personal guard. It continued to be an agonising trip, but the worst was behind me'.

Reeder eventually reached Hanoi and ended up in the infamous 'Hanoi Hilton' POW camp. He survived against all odds to be released at the end of the war. Later, having made contact with ex-VNAF personnel who had made it to the USA, he enquired about Xanh. Initially, Reeder struggled to locate him until he finally found a website that served as a gathering forum for former VNAF A-1 pilots. Eventually, through this site, he was reunited with Xanh;

'At our first encounter, I looked upon an older man, but instantly I saw the soul of my beloved friend in his eyes. I'd not seen him since I'd watched him forced across that log and marched away, knowing that I owed him

my life, or what there was left of it. But there in the jungle I made a promise to myself and to Xanh. Since he'd worked so hard to help me live through those two toughest days of my life, I felt like I owed him my very best to try to do my part to make his efforts worthwhile – to survive the rest of my journey and somehow get home at the end of it. What he'd done for me saved my life, and Xanh's selfless actions gave me even more determination to overcome everything between me and the freedom that waited at the end of my captivity.

'Nguyen Dinh Xanh has always been a great man, and now he is a great American. I am so thankful he was my friend when I needed him, and I am grateful I have found my friend again.'

Xanh's A-1 was one of 23 Skyraiders lost by the 530th FS between 1970 and mid-1973 – data does not extend beyond the latter date, so its losses were almost certainly higher. The unit also had six pilots killed or listed as missing in action.

In October 1974, with shortages of fuel, ordnance and spare parts, the 530th FS was ordered to cease operations. Pleiku AB was evacuated by the VNAF on 17 March 1975. Left behind were 21 A-1s and 18 other VNAF aircraft, all of which were in flyable condition.

6th ACS

Initially formed in World War 2 as the 6th FS(C), the 6th ACS was reconstituted at Hurlburt Field in 1962 under the control of the 1st ACW. Initially equipped with T-28s, the squadron moved to England AFB, Louisiana, along with its parent unit (1st ACW), in October 1967.

A-1H 137554 arrived in-theatre in September 1968 and subsequently served with the 6th ACS until the unit disbanded in 1969. During its time at Pleiku the Skyraider wore both ET and 6T codes, the latter shown here. The 6T code is thought to have been originally used by A-1s deployed by the unit to Da Nang to support the 'Spad' detachment there. However, over time, the unit's aircraft moved so often between the two locations that the 6T code lost its meaning. This A-1H was transferred to the VNAF in November 1970, and it became a combat loss on 12 June 1971 whilst serving with the 530th FS (*Jake Ludwig*)

Weapons loaders lift a 500-lb napalm tank onto Station 7 of A-1H 137552 in 1968. Note the wooden 'fillet' on the front of the MJ-1 'jammer' that held the napalm at the correct angle so the lugs on the weapon could engage the bomb rack. Note also that the SUU-11 mini-gun next to the napalm is lacking its front fairing, thus exposing the inner workings of the weapon. The tail of this Skyraider was painted in a 'one-of-a-kind' scheme modelled on the colours worn by French-built SPAD scouts of World War 1 (*Jake Ludwig*)

The A-1H/J Skyraiders that would equip the squadron were slow in reaching Louisiana. In late 1967 the Sacramento Air Materiel Area (SMAMA) at McClellan AFB, California, identified a total of 110 A-1H/Js suitable for transferring from the US Navy to the USAF. Its schedule indicated that the Naval Air Rework Facility (NARF) at NAS Quonset Point, Rhode Island, would modify 48 A-1H/Js (presumably including those earmarked for the 6th ACS) by March 1968. Eight of these Skyraiders were already in storage at NARF, but most were located in the Military Aircraft Storage and Disposition Center at Davis-Monthan AFB, Arizona. The aircraft would first be taken out of storage and flown to Rhode Island. Upon completion of modification to USAF standard, they would be flown to McClellan AFB and later transported to a port on the west coast for shipment to Vietnam.

The 6th ACS's initial cadre of pilots began arriving at Engalnd AFB in late 1967, but with the unit then lacking permanently assigned aircraft, the only flying they could do was the ferrying of A-1s from Davis-Monthan to Rhode Island, and later from Rhode Island to California. Modification of the squadron's first eight Skyraiders was completed by year-end, so pilots could finally begin flying training sorties in order to familiarise themselves with the handling qualities of the 6th ACS's 'new' single-seat Skyraiders.

Among the aviators checking in in January 1968 were veteran A-1 pilots Majs Win DePoorter and James 'Bob' Gochnauer. DePoorter had flown a previous combat tour with the 1st ACS at Bien Hoa AB in 1965-66, where he had completed about 350 combat missions. Gochnauer, who

later became known at 'Mr A-1' because of his 3500 hours in the Skyraider, had just come from an assignment at Hurlburt Field, where he had served as an A-1 instructor pilot teaching both USAF and VNAF pilots to fly the aircraft.

Shortly after their arrival at England AFB, they spotted two newly NARF-refurbished A-1Hs parked on the ramp with fresh coats of camouflage paint. Having their flight gear with them, they decided that the right thing to do was take these beauties up for a flight. The pilots coordinated a range time at nearby Claiborne Range and found some maintenance personnel to load the aircraft with practice ordnance.

Taking off in formation, they headed out to the training area to burn off some fuel prior to their range time commencing. After they had dropped their bombs on target, the pair headed back to the base and executed a flawless formation landing. Both men were amazed at the differences between the A-1H and the A-1E, just as we all were following our first flight in the single-seat version of the Skyraider. Both visibility and agility were greatly improved in the H-model. The most interesting part of this story, however, is the fact that this impromptu bombing mission had actually been the first flight that Gochnauer and DePoorter had made in the A-1H!

In late February 1968 the men of the 6th ACS, led by their CO, Lt Col Wallace Ford, boarded three C-141 Starlifters bound for Vietnam. Following a refuelling stop at Elmendorf AFB, Alaska, the Starlifters arrived at Pleiku AB on 1 March. Here, the men were greeted by Lt Col Norman Repp, the new commander of the 6th ACS! Needless to say, this revelation was a setback for the closely knit 6th ACS.

Carrying a mixed load of CBUs, napalm and WP bombs, A-1H 137520 is ready to go as the crew chief helps the pilot get properly strapped in. Once the latter is secure in his seat, he will don his helmet, grab his map and 'pubs' bag and be ready to crank the engine. This aircraft was declared a combat loss on 19 July 1969 at Da Nang when the pilot, while landing after declaring an emergency, was forced to leave the runway to avoid colliding with an airliner that had inexplicably been cleared for takeoff in the midst of his recovery! (*Mike Roberts*)

Cleveland Plain Dealer photo-journalist Mike Roberts rode in the right seat with Capt Randy Smedley on a 10 May 1968 mission. He took this photograph of their wingman as they flew to their target at Polei Klang. Seen here loaded with eight Mk 82 GP bombs, A-1E 133883 was hit by groundfire during its third pass on a VC target northwest of Phu Cat on 23 July 1969. The starboard wing burst into flames and the aircraft crashed before either Majs Franklin W Picking or Thomas H McCarty could escape (*Mike Roberts*)

Just prior to their arrival, the 1st ACS had moved from Pleiku AB to its new facility at Nakhon Phanom RTAFB. The leadership at Seventh Air Force had decided that it would be good if a small group of personnel (both maintainers and pilots) with Skyraider combat experience in Vietnam stayed behind to get the 6th ACS up to speed as quickly as possible. Lt Col Repp was promised the command of the incoming squadron if he agreed to stay. Since he outranked Lt Col Ford, he was given command. Like the good airman he was, Ford accepted the position as operations officer and went about his work. But squadron morale had been badly affected, and it took some time for this change to sink in. The men loved Lt Col Ford, and it was not easy to see him lose command of his unit.

The primary mission of the 6th ACS was to support American ground forces in the II Corps area of South Vietnam. The unit was to work particularly closely with the American Special Forces Studies and Observation Group (SOG), which operated as part of Program *Prairie Fire*.

SOG assets relied on helicopters to insert troops behind enemy lines, patrols then being extracted in a similar way. The A-1s of the 6th ACS, using the radio call-sign 'Spad', were the perfect assets to provide protection and reactionary fire should the SOG teams and/or their helicopter transport come under fire during either the insertion or extraction phase of the mission. Skyraiders were placed on alert and could be airborne within 15 minutes of notification should they be needed.

Pleiku AB was ideally situated to support this mission, being located near the Tri-Border area (conversion of Laos, Cambodia and South Vietnam), where much of the action took place. The SOG teams' primary task was to infiltrate areas where they could observe and report on troop movements and buildups. Should the team be detected and engaged, it would seek immediate extraction. These missions were always dangerous, especially for the extraction helicopter.

One of the handful of pilots who joined the 6th ACS upon its arrival at Pleiku was Capt Randy Smedley. 'When your name is "Smedley" you have to expect the worst', he told the author. 'As soon as I arrived at Pleiku, I became "Airman Smedley". I joined the "Spads" in 1968, and it didn't take long for me to be given that nickname'. Randy Smedley had settled in well to his job as a Skyraider pilot with the 1st ACS, and had accumulated about 300 hours of combat time with the unit prior to transferring to the newly arrived 6th ACS.

On 10 May 1968, Smedley arrived at squadron operations to get ready for his mission. He was notified that he would be flying an A-1E on this occasion, as he would be carrying a passenger in the form of a newspaper reporter. As Smedley was getting ready for the mission, up walked Mike Roberts, a photo-journalist working for the *Cleveland Plain Dealer*. Smedley would be leading a two-ship formation on a CAS mission to the central highlands of South Vietnam. Roberts eventually ended up being in Vietnam on assignment for a full year, but the events of this day would trump the rest of his tour.

'Spad 27' flight took off and flew west to Polei Klang, where friendly forces were in trouble and needed help. The 'Spads' were soon on station and received a briefing from the FAC, who told them that there was a

A-1H 134569 of the 22nd SOS patrols the skies in June 1969 during a day mission, probably over Laos. The mixed load of six Mk 81 'Ladyfingers' and six Mk 82s makes for an interesting combination. The 250-lb Mk 81 could be dropped closer to friendly positions than the larger Mk 82, making it a slightly better weapon for CAS. Notice the black 300-gallon tank and black lettering on the tail (*Ed Homan*)

friendly patrol that had been ambushed and was pinned down. Once the FAC had marked the target the A-1s went to work. Roberts hung on as best he could, definitely getting more than he bargained for. After five passes, the 'Spads' were out of bombs. That was when things got interesting.

The FAC said there was a 0.51-cal machine gun raking fire over the pinned down patrol. The 'Spads' were asked if they could help. Smedley knew that duelling with guns was a losing proposition, but the guys on the ground were desperate. Having been in a very similar situation myself, I understand completely when operational necessity overrides 'common sense'. The 'Spads' rolled in and Roberts recalled what happened next;

'We came in firing our 20 mm guns at the tree line and the 0.51-cal answered. A tracer leapt in front of the aeroplane, and another over it, but the next one hit with a "thwack". There was a bright flash and I saw it deflect off the A-1 and into the air.'

Despite the battle damage, the 'Spads' made it home safely, and the friendly forces escaped the ambush. Roberts and Smedley looked at the damaged aeroplane, shook hands and parted ways. Each went in their separate directions and that was that, or was it? On 18 February 2012 I received an e-mail from Roberts asking if I knew a Randy Smedley. I knew he was on our SpadNet list, so I forwarded Roberts' e-mail to him. The two reconnected after nearly 44 years and relived that mission in Vietnam. I was happy to facilitate that reunion.

The 6th ACS (which became the 6th SOS on 1 August 1968) operated Skyraiders from late February 1968 to mid-November 1969. During this 21-month period it lost no fewer than 19 A-1s and had 12 pilots either killed or listed as MIA. One of the losses was due to a ground accident that resulted in the aircraft's destruction.

Thee 'Zorros' pose in front of their squadron sign in August 1969 at 'NKP'. 1Lt Ed Homan is flanked by Capt John Dyer and 1Lt 'Rip' Riopelle (*Ed Homan*)

22nd SOS

The very last USAF unit formed to fly the A-1 in Southeast Asia, the 22nd SOS commenced operations from 'NKP' in the autumn of 1968. The squadron's 'Zorro' call-sign and patch were inherited from the 606th ACS at 'NKP', which had flown AT-28Ds in the same night role that would now become the speciality of the 22nd SOS. The nocturnal interdiction mission over the Ho Chi Minh Trail would later be spread among other A-1 squadrons at 'NKP', but for a full year the night 'belonged' to the 'Zorros' of the 22nd SOS.

1Lt Ed Homan, who flew his fair share of missions after dark with the unit during 1969-70, recalled the following event that occurred during a night sortie he flew with a pilot he was checking out in an A-1E-5 (no controls for the right seat passenger);

'Rich got over to "NKP" late in my tour as I recall, and I was assigned as one of his IPs to get him checked out for night combat. The first ride he made with me came in an A-1E-5, and this version of the Skyraider really sucked for the poor IP who had to sit there with his hands in his lap. I was being "Mr Cool" checking out the new guy on his first night ride in *Steel Tiger* [interdiction operations over Laos]. As we were getting our briefing from the "Candle" FAC, I was calmly pointing out the AAA that was coming up all along the trail. "That's some 85 mm to the north of us", I said. "We aren't too concerned about that gun. It's rate-of-fire is too slow, and we can easily avoid the shells. The same goes for that 57 mm that's coming up in the area of Mu Gia Pass.

'"Even the numerous batteries firing 37 mm rounds that you are seeing are quite easy to avoid unless they really gang up on you". I was really feeling cocky giving the new guy a glimpse of what life was like

A 'Sandy' pilot in A-1H 134584 has his 'air conditioner' on 'high' as he escorts the Jolly Green during refuelling operations over Laos in 1969. This was during the period when all three squadrons in the 56th SOW shared all missions – SAR, night operations and *Prairie Fire* SOG support. This aircraft was transferred to the VNAF at the end of 1970, and there is no record of its loss (*Mike Maloney*)

on the trail at night. Our first couple of passes only bolstered my ego even more as we struck a truck convoy that was seemingly defended by a solitary 37 mm site that was easily avoided. My overconfidence quickly ebbed away, however, as we pulled up from our third run on the convoy. Two batteries armed with twin 23 mm cannon opened up on us from both sides of the pass. My voice went up so many octaves that I sounded like a little girl screaming "and those are twin 23mms! Jink left, no right, no back left" as I kept grabbing for the non-existent stick between my legs. The smell of cordite filled the cockpit, and neither of us could talk for a while. I suggested that we come in from a different direction, get rid of everything we had left and call it a night.

'After returning to base I went into the squadron commander's office the next day and suggested that no IP be assigned a "Dash-5" E-model again. He agreed that those aeroplanes should be flown solo only from then on.'

The ordnance load for 'truck hunting' missions on the trail was no different from that used during the day, with one major exception. Somewhere, the USAF had found a supply of incendiary bombs that were left over from World War 2. Sent to the ammunition dump at 'NKP', the weapons were referred to as 'funny bombs' by the A-1 pilots, although they were technically M36 incendiary bombs. Just a single weapon was loaded onto each of the inboard wing stubs as they weighed nearly 1000 lbs apiece.

A former 'Zorro' described what it was like to drop an M36;

'The "funny bombs" were like nothing else we carried. After release, the clamshell down the centre of the bomb opened up in flight and the bomblets spread out and ignited when they hit the ground (and hopefully the target). Over a period of five to ten seconds the number of igniting white-hot bomblets grew and grew until they formed an oval pattern.

All three A-1 squadrons at 'NKP' are represented in this photograph taken at a 'Sawatdee' party given in honour of those heading home after completing their one-year tours. Each squadron had coloured party suits – green for the 22nd SOS, orange for the 602nd SOS and blue for the 1st SOS. Pictured, from left to right, are Ken Brown, Jim Matthews, Ed Homan, Randy Bertrand, George Harvey and Mike Maloney (*Ed Homan*)

The bomblets were mesmerising, and they burned for five to eight minutes. Anything that happened to be hit by them was "toast". Secondaries were common, and a source of great delight! Watching "funny bombs" would have been even more enjoyable had it not been for all those nasty red streaks zipping by the canopy!'

Another A-1 pilot from the unit explained that 'when that thermite went off the FAC would have an orgasm. They glowed so brilliantly that if you looked at them your night vision would immediately revert to a sunny afternoon in downtown "NKP". It was like having a two million-candle power flare flying on your wing. Anything within the football field-sized oval that a single bomb covered would be incinerated. It was a great weapon'.

WELCOME TO 'NKP'

22nd SOS pilot Charlie Holder recalled the events that unfolded when he first arrived at 'NKP' to begin his A-1 tour;

'I remember clambering off the C-130 and immediately falling down on the wet, slick PSP that had been laid in the parking area. For the most part the "Zorros" got the "more senior" guys, but hey, I'd been a captain for almost a year so I became a "Zorro"!

'For us newbies our first combat mission was with an FAC over the Trail in daytime. Our FAC was an OV-10 "Nail", and we were socked in by weather for almost the entire time – I rarely saw the ground. From then on our entire ten-ride checkout was flown at night, with the first A-1 ride in the right seat and the next nine in the left!

'I do remember one funny story (at least now, in hindsight, it seems funny) from my first left seat ride. My checkout IP, Dick Novak, told me to make a pass and fire all of my rockets from the two LAU-19s we had on board. I dutifully reset the sight depression, re-checked my switches so I wouldn't drop the pods but would fire the rockets, acquired the target, set up the perch and rolled in. I tracked the target and everything looking good. Fire, and everything went black! The burning rocket exhaust from 38 folding-fin aerial rockets put out a LOT of light, and my night vision went away entirely. After Dick recovered the aeroplane from the unusual

The pilot of A-1H 139702 of the 22nd SOS flies with the canopy open. The airspeed limit for an open canopy in the A-1H/J was 180 KIAS (knots indicated airspeed). Normal cruise airspeed was about 140 knots for the Skyraider, with fuel consumption of about 1000 lbs per hour. Configured as shown, this A-1's mission length would be a bit under three hours. This aircraft was lost to small arms fire during its second pass against an enemy troop concentration target west of Khe Sanh on 28 July 1971. Maj D H Potton of the 1st SOS ejected moments prior to the Skyraider crashing, and he was soon rescued by a US Army helicopter (*Ed Homan*)

attitude I had put us into, he said "Now you know why you close your eyes when you fire rockets!" That was a lesson I never forgot.'

Former 22nd SOS pilot 2Lt Jim Partington also had a memorable first mission from 'NKP';

'My first "Zorro" mission was, of course, in the right seat. It was in the wet season and, as always, it was raining harder than I had ever seen before. So naturally I figured the only reason we were going down to the TUOC [Tactical Units Operations Center] to brief was because these guys wanted to show the new second lieutenant how they did things. I was sure we were going to weather cancel.

'Well we got there, soaking wet, and got the intel and weather briefings. Sure enough the intel was normal, and the weather was overcast from India to the Pacific, but I was getting to see how the old heads did things. By the way, all the fast mover sorties we were to have as assets had cancelled for weather. Next, we did the flight brief, in truly professional fashion for the second lieutenant's benefit, just like we were really going out to fly.

'The time came to man up the aircraft, and we even went out to the flightline. It was raining so hard that we could not see more than a couple of revetments at a time, and the water on the oil-slicked PSP was almost over my once spit-shined flying boots. Man, were these guys putting on a show for the FNG [Fucking New Guy]!

'Following a brief pre-flight inspection, and three attempts by me to climb up on the extra oil-coated right wing, we were in the machine. I was guessing that they would call it off after they showed me how the pre-flight and check-in was done here in the war. We did that and started the beast! Did I say it was raining? In fact I did not think it could rain *inside* an aircraft that hard!

This photograph provides a good close look at A-1H 139810 upon its return from a mission in 1969. Note the 'special' leather flying helmet worn by Ed Homan, which he had donned to mark his finé flight and, therefore, the completion of his tour. It was customary to celebrate this occurrence with a bit of flamboyance, as it was a momentous occasion. A traditional 'hose down' from the fire trucks and the sharing of champagne with squadron members awaiting the honoree's arrival were all part of the 'programme' (*Ed Homan*)

'We were going to taxi – I guess you had to show the ground troops that we needed them to work in all that rain. The visibility was just good enough to keep from chopping lead's tail off on the way to the arming area. They pulled the pins too – those poor arming crews had to feel needed, but soon they would put the pins in so that we could call it a night. I didn't think that I would ever dry off. Running the machines up was a nice touch – got to get those engines good and warm if you want them to start again in all this water. Upon calling the tower they confirmed that the visibility and crosswinds were both at our limits. Then the leader took off, and we followed – these guys were not kidding!

'We did not see lead again until an hour later over the "PDJ" [Plaines des Jarres], or so my pilot said – he could not prove it to me. All I saw was solid undercast from horizon to horizon, just as the weatherman had said. We made a weather check for about an hour and saw no glimpse of the ground. Then the leader told us to take 1000-ft altitude spacing and head back south directly at the wall of thunderstorms that we had just barely survived – in my opinion – on the way up there. We got back over "NKP" intact, with all our bombs and bullets, against all odds. Our reward was a heavyweight night approach to minimums, and then a gusty crosswind landing on a runway covered with standing water.

'I had just watched a pilot do what I was sure was impossible in an A-1, and I knew that no ops officer would have cleared the mission had he known about it. My instructor, who happened to BE the 22nd SOS's ops officer, topped it off after the debrief by saying "tomorrow night, you get to do it". And of course he made me do just that.'

Based exclusively at 'NKP' throughout its time in-theatre, the 22nd SOS lost nine aircraft and two pilots between October 1968 and September 1970.

A-1H 135273 makes its way from Cam Ranh Bay AB to 'NKP' in late January 1968. Note the lack of tail markings except for the aircraft serial number. An A-1 would be assigned to a specific squadron upon the aircraft's arrival at its frontline base. At this time there were four USAF A-1 squadrons in Southeast Asia, and this aircraft would end up at Pleiku in service with the 6th SOS. It was a combat loss on 17 December 1969, by which time the A-1 was serving with the 22nd SOS (*Gordon Fornell*)

APPENDICES

USAF A-1 UNITS IN VIETNAM

1st Air Commando Squadron (Composite) (17 June 1963), later 1st Air Commando Squadron, (Fighter) (15 August 1967), later 1st Special Operations Squadron (1 August 1968)
Call-signs – 'Hobo', 'Sandy' and 'Spad' (when TDY to Pleiku and Da Nang from late 1969 to December 1970)
Tail markings – EC and 6T at Pleiku, TC at Nakhon Phanom
Next higher HQ – 34th TG (8 July 1963 to 7 July 1965), 6251st TFW (7 July 1965 to 21 November 1965), 3rd TFW (21 November 1965 to 8 March 1966), 14th ACW (8 March 1966 to 19 December 1967), 56th ACW, later 56th SOW (20 December 1967 to 14 December 1972)
Base(s) – flew Skyraiders from Bien Hoa (detachment at Qui Nhon) from June 1964 to January 1966, Pleiku from January 1966 to December 1967 and Nakhon Phanom from December 1967 to November 1972

602nd Fighter Squadron (Commando) (1 May 1963), reconstituted 18 October 1964 and later 602nd SOS (1 August 1968)
Call-signs – 'Firefly', 'Sandy', 'Spad' and 'Dragonfly'
Tail markings – TT at Udorn and Nakhon Phanom
Next higher HQ – 34th TG (8 July 1963 to 7 July 1965), 6251st TFW (8 July 1965 to 21 November 1965), 3rd TFW (21 November 1965 to 8 March 1966), 56th ACW, later 56th SOW (8 March 1966 to 31 December 1970)
Base(s) – flew Skyraiders from Bien Hoa (detachment at Qui Nhon) from October 1964 to January 1966, Nha Trang from February 1966 to December 1966, Udorn from December 1966 to June 1968 and Nakhon Phanom from 1 July 1968 to 31 December 1970

6th Air Commando Squadron (28 February 1968), later 6th SOS (1 August 1968)
Call sign – 'Spad'
Tail markings – ET and 6T at Pleiku
Next higher HQ – 633rd TFW
Base – flew Skyraiders from Pleiku (detachment at Da Nang) until 15 November 1969

22nd Special Operations Squadron (25 October 1968)
Call-signs – 'Zorro' and 'Sandy'
Tail markings – TS at Nakhon Phanom
Next higher HQ – 56th SOW
Base – flew Skyraiders from Nakhon Phanom until 30 September 1970

Hurlburt A-1 Training Units – 603rd FS(C) (1 July 1963), later 603rd ACS, stopped A-1 training on April 1966; 604th FS(C) (1 July 63 to 8 November 1964); 4409th CCTS (8 November 1964 to late 1967); 4407th CCTS (November 1967 to November 1972)
Call-sign – various
Tail markings – AD until late 1971, then AH
Next higher HQ – 1st ACW, re-designated 1st SOW on 1 August 1968
Base – all referenced units operated Skyraiders from Hurlburt Field (Eglin AFB Auxiliary Field No 9) until October 1972

VNAF A-1 UNITS

1st Fighter Squadron (initially established on 1 June 1956 and received AD-6 Skyraiders in September 1960), later redesignated 514th FS (17 June 1963)
Call-sign – 'Phoenix' (Phoung Hoang)
Markings – 514th Phoenix insignia on cowl and various markings on tail
Next higher HQ – 23rd TW at Bien Hoa
Base – flew Skyraiders from Bien Hoa until 24 April 1975

516th Fighter Squadron (initially established in December 1961 as 2nd FS and received first Skyraiders in May 1964 after redesignation to 516th FS)
Call-sign – 'Tiger' (Phi Ho)
Markings – 516th Tiger insignia on cowl and small 'p' on tail
Next higher HQ – 41st TW at Da Nang
Base – flew Skyraiders from Da Nang until early 1969

518th Fighter Squadron (15 October 1963)
Call-sign – 'Dragon' (Phi Long)
Markings – 518th Dragon insignia on cowl and small 'k' on tail
Next higher HQ – 23rd TW at Bien Hoa
Base – flew Skyraiders from Bien Hoa until 29 April 1975

520th Fighter Squadron (16 June 1964)
Call-sign – 'Panther' (Than Bao)
Markings – 520th Panther on cowl and small 'v' on tail
Next higher HQ – 74th TW at Binh Thuy
Base(s) – flew Skyraiders from Bien Hoa and then Binh Thuy until 1 May 1969

524th Fighter Squadron (established December 1961 and received first Skyraiders on 15 September 1965)
Call-sign – 'Thunder' (Thien Loi)
Markings – 524th insignia on cowl and small 'z' on tail; later 524th insignia on fuselage
Next higher HQ – 62nd TW at Nha Trang
Base(s) – flew Skyraiders from Nha Trang from September 1965, with a detachment at Pleiku from 1966 to 1968; converted to A-37s in early 1969

530th Fighter Squadron (established 1970)
Call-sign – 'Jupiter' (Thai Duong)
Markings – no insignia on cowl, unknown on tail
Next higher HQ – 72nd TW at Pleiku
Base – flew Skyraiders from Cu Hanh until October 1974

83rd Special Air Group (formed early 1964)
Call-sign – 'Than Phong'
Markings – Cuu Sac insignia on cowl, Than Phong emblem on fuselage and large U on tail
Next higher HQ – VNAF HQ
Base – flew Skyraiders from Tan Son Nhut AB until January 1968

TIMELINE

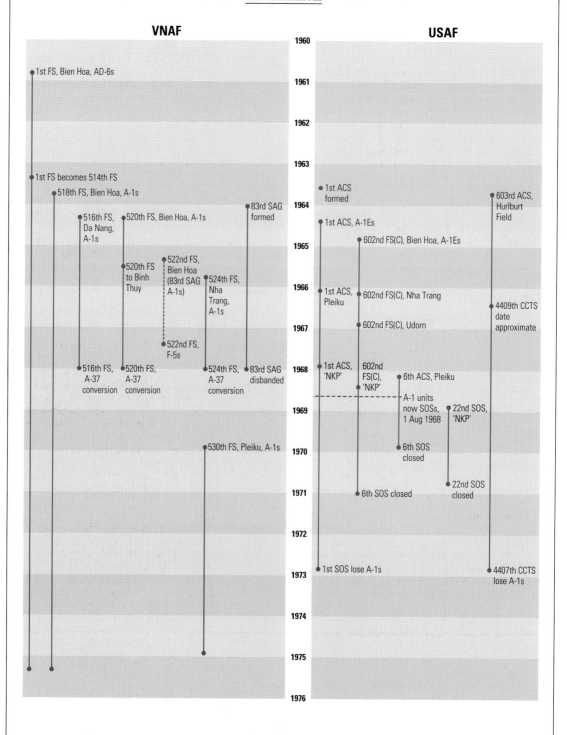

VNAF

1960

1st FS, Bien Hoa, AD-6s

1961

1962

1963

1st FS becomes 514th FS

518th FS, Bien Hoa, A-1s

83rd SAG formed

1964

516th FS, Da Nang, A-1s

520th FS, Bien Hoa, A-1s

1965

520th FS to Binh Thuy

522nd FS, Bien Hoa (83rd SAG A-1s)

524th FS, Nha Trang, A-1s

1966

1967

522nd FS, F-5s

516th FS, A-37 conversion

520th FS, A-37 conversion

524th FS, A-37 conversion

83rd SAG disbanded

1968

1969

530th FS, Pleiku, A-1s

1970

1971

1972

1973

1974

1975

1976

USAF

1st ACS formed

603rd ACS, Hurlburt Field

1st ACS, A-1Es

602nd FS(C), Bien Hoa, A-1Es

1st ACS, Pleiku

602nd FS(C), Nha Trang

4409th CCTS date approximate

602nd FS(C), Udorn

1st ACS, 'NKP'

602nd FS(C), 'NKP'

6th ACS, Pleiku

A-1 units now SOSs, 1 Aug 1968

22nd SOS, 'NKP'

6th SOS closed

22nd SOS closed

6th SOS closed

1st SOS lose A-1s

4407th CCTS lose A-1s

COLOUR PLATES

1

A-1E 132637 of the 602nd FS(C), Bien Hoa AB, Republic of Vietnam, 1964

Although marked with the roundel of the VNAF, this aircraft was in fact a USAF Skyraider. Its mission load consists of Mk 76 practice bombs. Despite the seeming contradiction of training ordnance in a war zone, this was an important first role for USAF Skyraider units in Vietnam. This aircraft suffered a technical malfunction whilst on a test flight on 26 December 1965, the A-1 crashing near Bien Hoa. Its pilot, Maj Lewis R Raleigh, was killed.

2

A-1H 135256 of the 514th, Bien Hoa AB, Republic of Vietnam, September 1964

Laden with old-style GP bombs and unguided rockets, this VNAF A-1H is configured for a strike mission against enemy forces in South Vietnam. It is believed that the Satan-style art denotes its assignment to one of the flights within the 514th FS. Stylised markings such as these were unique to this period, and they were gone by 1965. This aircraft was lost on 6 April 1965.

3

A-1E 133914 of the 602nd FS(C), Bien Hoa AB, Republic of Vietnam, 1965

This VNAF-marked A-1E from the 34th TG is depicted here with a mission load of six 500- and two 750-lb napalm tanks. At this early stage of the conflict the aircraft would have been crewed by a USAF pilot and a VNAF observer, the latter to coordinate with the FAC and/or ground forces as needed. 133914 was downed by AAA over southern Laos on 4 March 1970, although its pilot, Capt D E Friestad, was rescued.

4

A-1H 134610 of the 83rd SAG, Bien Hoa AB, Republic of Vietnam, 1966

The 83rd SAG was the elite unit of the VNAF that was formed in early 1964. This A-1H is adorned with the group's special markings, as well as the unique cowl marking Cuu Sach (this translates to 'The Better' in English). Borrowed from the 522nd FS, 134610's final fate remains unknown.

5

A-1H 135281 of the 518th FS, Bien Hoa AB, Republic of Vietnam, 1965

135281 sports an early US Navy style paint scheme. VNAF Skyraiders with markings and ordnance loads such as this participated in the first strike against North Vietnamese targets on 8 February 1965 as part of Operation *Flaming Dart*. No loss record exists for this aircraft.

6

A-1H 137569 of the 520th FS, Binh Thuy AB, Republic of Vietnam, 1966

This A-1H carries a full load of ordnance, which was something of a rarity for VNAF Skyraiders later in the war when bomb shortages forced partial loads that saw at least half of the external stations empty. But more ordnance usually meant more delivery passes, increasing the already high threat faced by A-1 pilots as enemy gunners became more proficient. No loss record exists for this aircraft.

7

A-1E 132649 of the 1st ACS, Pleiku AB, Republic of Vietnam, 10 March 1966

The mount of Maj Bernie Fisher during his Medal of Honor mission to A-Shau Valley, 132649 is depicted here as it was configured on 10 March 1966. This CAS load of ten M30 100-lb GP bombs and two M47 100-lb white phosphorous bombs and 800 rounds of 20 mm ammunition was lethal, yet it was flexible enough to allow delivery within 100 metres of friendly troops. The 150-gallon Centreline Fuel Tank provided the extended range and loiter time necessary for this mission. 132649 is on permanent display at the National Museum of the Air Force at Wright-Patterson AFB, Ohio.

8

A-1E 132582 of the 1st ACS, Pleiku AB, Republic of Vietnam, 1967

This Skyraider displays the 'new' Southeast Asian style paint scheme adopted by the USAF from late 1965, along with its two-letter EC code that confirmed the aircraft was assigned to the 1st ACS 'Hobos' at Pleiku. Mk 82 high drag (Snakeye) bombs, as seen here, were designed to increase separation between the aircraft and the exploding weapon, which would detonate upon impact with the ground. Snakeyes were not common ordnance for Skyraiders, being more suited to 'fast movers' that needed to get closer to the target to gain acceptable results. No loss record exists for this aircraft.

9

A-1G 132528 of the 1st ACS, Pleiku AB, Republic of Vietnam, 1967

This aircraft had a remarkable history, both beginning and ending its Vietnam War experience with the VNAF. In between, it was part of the USAF Skyraider fleet, operating from Pkeiku AB and, later, Nakhon Phanom RTAFB with the 1st SOS. The emblem of the VNAF's 516th FS remained on the A-1's cowl for some unknown reason, despite its reassignment to the USAF. 132528 was one of 11 Skyraiders to be flown to U-Tapao RTAFB when South Vietnam was invaded in April 1975.

10

A-1H 137564 of the 524th FS, Nha Trang AB, Republic of Vietnam, 1966

The 524th FS was based at Nha Trang with its Skyraiders from September 1965 to early 1969, when it converted to the A-37. As with all A-1s issued to the VNAF from US Navy stocks, this aircraft has no tailhook. Skyraiders received later through MAP retained their tailhooks. No loss record exists for this aircraft.

11

A-1E 132444 of the 602nd FS(C), Udorn RTAFB, Thailand, 11 November 1967

Lt Col Ralph 'Tad' Hoggatt flew this aircraft, configured as shown, on a 'Sandy' mission to rescue downed airmen (one of whom was 1Lt Lance Sijan, who was posthumously awarded the Medal of Honor for his devotion to duty as a POW) on 11 November 1967. Despite heavy and accurate enemy ground fire that downed his wingman (Maj William C Griffith, flying A-1E 132569) and damaged his own aircraft, Hoggatt orchestrated the recovery of his squadronmate. For his actions on that day, Hoggatt, who completed 204 combat missions, was awarded the Air Force Cross. 132444 subsequently became a MAP transfer to the VNAF on 12 October 1970 and was eventually lost on 31 March 1971.

12

A-1E-5 135211 of the 602nd FS(C), Nakhon Phanom RTAFB, Thailand, 1968

Tropic Moon (TM) was a programme initiated to test an early night-attack capability using the A-1. By most accounts, this was a successful trial that led to future development of USAF night-attack capability. TM aircraft were returned to their original condition following completion of the year-long test. This aircraft was lost to AAA near Ban Ban during a *Barrel Roll* strike on 11 November 1969, its pilot, Capt G H Porter, being rescued a short while later by an HH-53 from the 40th Air Rescue and Recovery Squadron (ARRS).

13

A-1H 134609 of the 6th ACS, Pleiku AB, Republic of Vietnam, 1967

Nicknamed *BAD NEWS*, this A-1 is loaded with 'hard ordnance', indicating that it has been prepared for an interdiction mission where the close proximity of 'friendlies' to enemy forces will not be a factor. The 'Daisy Cutter' fuse extenders seen here were used to ensure that the bombs would detonate before being buried in the soft earth. CBUs of this type were not typically carried by the Skyraider. The 6T tail code (also unique) was originally used by 6th ACS aircraft serving at Da Nang. This aircraft was a MAP transfer to the VNAF, and it was lost on 12 November 1972 – less than three weeks after being handed over to the South Vietnamese.

14

A-H 134520 of the 6th SOS, Pleiku AB, Republic of Vietnam, 1968

The epitome of a specialised ordnance load, this A-1H has been loaded with 144 fragmentation bombs weighing 20 lbs each. Designed for use against personnel or materiel, these weapons proved highly effective when employed against massed enemy concentrations. This aircraft survived its time with the USAF and was transferred to the VNAF in the autumn of 1970, with whom it was subsequently lost on 18 January 1973.

15

A-1H 139802 of the 516th FS, Da Nang AB, Republic of Vietnam, 1966

A seeming contradiction of stealth and flamboyance, this A-1H supported ARVN forces in I Corps from its base in Da Nang.

The unique VNAF camouflage style seen on 139802 would change to the standard Southeast Asian scheme in 1967. Even then, however, the high-visibility emblems and fuselage bands synonymous with early VNAF A-1s would remain on some Skyraiders. This aircraft was lost on 7 December 1970.

16

A-1H 139608 of the 1st SOS, Nakhon Phanom RTAFB, Thailand, 1968

BLOOD, SWEAT & TEARS was named by 1Lt Bert Bertrand of the 1st SOS after his love for the rock band of the same name. Its non-subdued ordnance stands out in stark contrast to the rest of the aeroplane. Later, the tan outline applied to the tail markings would be changed to white, and stores carried under the wings would become mostly olive drab in colour. This aircraft survived its USAF service, and there is no record of its loss whilst with the VNAF.

17

A-1H 137570 of the 524th FS, Nha Trang AB, Republic of Vietnam, 1968-69

This uniquely marked Skyraider was assigned to the 524th FS at Nha Trang – the fuselage emblem was one of two used by this squadron. Unlike VNAF A-1s from earlier times, this one carries less than half of its allowable load. Lack of external fuel tanks would indicate relatively short distances from base to target. 137570 was lost on 3 November 1969.

18

A-1J 142056 of the 602nd SOS, Nakhon Phanom RTAFB, Thailand, 1969

TINY TIM is armed with dual 7.62 mm miniguns, eight CBUs, two napalm tanks and 800 rounds of 20 mm ammunition – a lethal and persistent CAS load. In later years 100-lb WP bombs replaced napalm, thus improving the Skyraider's agility. This aircraft was transferred to the VNAF in the spring of 1971 and was lost on 20 December that same year.

19

A-1E 133878 of the 22nd SOS, Nakhon Phanom RTAFB, Thailand, 1968-70

ORIENT EXPRESS was a night intruder with the 'Zorros' of the 22nd SOS. Its ordnance load was tailored to interdict trucks travelling along the Ho Chi Minh Trail. The M36 incendiary bomb, seen here on the inner wing pylon, was commonly referred to as a 'funny bomb'. It was filled with 182 thermite bomblets that proved very effective against trucks. This aircraft, which participated in the Son Tay Raid on 20/21 November 1970, was transferred to the VNAF in November 1972. No loss records exist for it.

20

A-1H 134488 of the 516th FS, Da Nang AB, Republic of Vietnam, 1970

By 1970 the supply of old-style GP bombs had been exhausted, and newer low drag GP (LDGP) bombs were being used almost exclusively by both the USAF and VNAF. The six empty wing stations on this aircraft are offset somewhat by the M117 GP 750-lb bombs on the inboard stations. 134488 was a combat loss on 8 October 1972.

21
A-1E 132686 of the 4407th CCTS, Hurlburt Field, Florida, 1968

This A-1E was part of the Skyraider training fleet at Hurlburt Field in the late 1960s. Conservatively, 98 per cent of the USAF pilots who flew Skyraiders were trained at Hurlburt Field. Although this aircraft is carrying inert training ordnance, a loadout such as this gave new Skyraider pilots a flavour of what it was like to fly a 23,000-lb single-engined, propeller-driven aircraft. 132686 made it to the war zone when it was transferred to the VNAF in November 1972. The aircraft's final fate is unknown.

22
A-1J 142014 of the 530th FS, Pleiku AB, Republic of Vietnam, 1971

This Skyraider exemplifies a much more subdued and conservative camouflage scheme as opposed to earlier examples from the VNAF. It is loaded with Mk 81 LDGP 'Ladyfingers', their slender, diminutive size leading to their nickname. The presence of a tailhook on 142014 indicates that it came to the VNAF as a MAP transfer from the USAF. The aircraft was lost on 30 September 1971.

23
A-1H 137628 of the 22nd SOS, Da Nang AB, Republic of Vietnam, December 1969

Decorated with a 'sharksmouth', this Skyraider was one of the 'Sandy' alert aircraft at Da Nang while on duty with Operating Location Alpha Alpha, which was in turn part of the 56th SOW. Designed to poke fun at the co-located 366th TFW 'Gunfighters' and their 'sharksmouth' F-4Ds, the design was short lived on the A-1 – it was removed after the aircraft's return to 'NKP'. 137628 was lost over Laos on 9 April 1971 during a SAR mission for a ground reconnaissance team, resulting in the death of Capt Carroll B Lilly.

24
A-1J 142072 of the 56th SOW, Nakhon Phanom RTAFB, Thailand, 1971

Undoubtedly the most photographed Skyraider at 'NKP', A-1J 142072 often provided the backdrop for official photographs featuring squadron personnel. It crash landed at Udorn RTAFB following battle damage on 27 December 1968 and was later transported to 'NKP' to be repaired. Marked up erroneously as 'FR 587', none of us knew that it would become the only A-1J known to have survived the war. Its true identity (142072) was recently determined during restoration at the Thai Air Force Museum in Bangkok, Thailand, where it now resides.

25
A-1E 133892 of the 514th FS, Bien Hoa AB, Republic of Vietnam, 1972

By this late stage of the war, the VNAF did not have to fly far from Bien Hoa AB in order to find NVA forces that were engaging ARVN troops in III Corps. This aircraft's load of eight Mk 82 LDGP bombs was more suited to interdiction as opposed to CAS for friendly forces, however. 133892 was lost on 18 January 1973 – the same day as A-1H 134520, featured in Profile 14.

26
A-1G 133865 of the 1st SOS, Nakhon Phanom RTAFB, Thailand, 1972

This A-1G from the 1st SOS 'Hobos' was flown in this configuration by 1Lt Tex Brown on a *Barrel Roll* mission in early 1972. On 2 May that same year, whilst being flown by Maj Jim Harding as part of a flight of two 'Hobos' supporting friendly ground forces just south of the DMZ, both Skyraiders (the other aircraft was A-1E-5 135141, flown by Capt D R Screws) were shot down by SA-7 'Strella' shoulder-launched SAMs. These were the second and third USAF A-1s lost to the SA-7. Both pilots were rescued.

27
A-1H 135332 of the 4407th CCTS, Hurlburt Field, Florida, 1971

The ordnance load carried by this A-1H was ideal for training students in ground attack techniques and procedures from Hurlburt Field. New A-1 pilots practised rocket, bomb, napalm and strafe deliveries under controlled conditions. This aircraft was a MAP transfer in mid-June 1972, and it was one of the 11 Skyraiders flown to U-Tapao on 29 April 1975. 135332 was returned to the USA for eventual display in the National Air and Space Museum in Washington, DC.

28
A-1H 135340 of the 514th FS, Bien Hoa AB, Republic of Vietnam, 1971

This A-1H from the 514th FS shows a variation of previously seen camouflage schemes for VNAF Skyraiders. The national flag is absent from the tail, there is no cowl marking, nor VNAF roundel on the fuselage. The ordnance load of mixed Mk 81 and Mk 82 LDGPs was a flexible configuration for a variety of target types. This aircraft was lost on 28 March 1973.

29
A-1H 139665 of the 1st SOS, Nakhon Phanom RTAFB, Thailand, 1972

LIEUTENANT AMERICA was the mount of 1Lt Randy Scott of the 1st SOS 'Hobos', the A-1H being configured in the standard 'Sandy' load of this period. It was transferred to the VNAF in November 1972, where it served with the 514th FS. 139665 was flown to Thailand on 29 April 1975 and then returned to the USA. It has since been restored to flying condition and is based at the Tennessee Museum of Aviation.

30
A-1H 139738 of the 1st SOS, Nakhon Phanom RTAFB, Thailand, 1972

THE PROUD AMERICAN is depicted here as it looked when it became the final USAF Skyraider to be lost during the Vietnam War on 28 September 1972 whilst being flown over northern Laos by 1Lt Lance Smith – he was rescued by an Air America helicopter. Earlier, this had been the aircraft flown by Lt Col William Jones, commander of the 602nd SOS, on his Medal of Honor mission of 1 September 1968. His heroic actions on that day led to the safe recovery of a downed US airman. The name 'The Proud American' was first used on A-1H 134555 by Capt Don Combs.

INDEX

References to illustrations are shown in **bold**.
Plates are shown with page and caption locators in brackets.